RESOURCING
CLASSROO
DRAMA: 8-1

Mark Cremin
& Teresa Grainger

NATE

ACKNOWLEDGEMENTS

We would like to thank all the children and teachers who contributed to the creation of this book, through their involvement in these dramas. In particular, the headteacher Vivienne Resch and staff at The Slade CP School Tonbridge, as well as colleagues at St. Stephens RCP Bexley, Langdon School London Borough of Newham, Northend CP Thamesmead, Belvedere CP Bexley, Holy Trinity RCP Margate and Cedaroak Elementary School, Portland, Oregon, U.S.A. Also, Ann Shreeve, NATE's Publications Officer for her tolerance, support and advice, and Jo Bradbury for her photographs. We are additionally indebted to the many teachers we have worked with on in-service courses, and those who have welcomed us into their classrooms to teach their children. Finally, to our children Patrick and Lucy who also deserve our love and thanks for the time they have missed with us during the writing of this book.

PERMISSIONS

We are grateful to the following for permissions to reproduce illustrations:

Blodin The Beast by Michael Morpurgo and Christina Balit: Francis Lincoln Ltd, 4 Torriano Mews, Torriano Avenue, London, NW5 2RU
The Boy and the Cloth of Dreams by Jenny Caralek: Walker Books Ltd
Little Wolf's Book of Badness by Ian Whybrow, illustrated by Tony Ross: Harper Collins,
The Green Children by Kevin Crossley-Holland and Alan Marks: Alan Marks
The Hairy Hands by Gene Kemp: Penguin UK
Auntie Dot's Incredible Adventure Atlas: Harper Collins
Tapestry of Tales, Sandra Palmer and Elisabeth Brouilly: Harper Collins
The Highwayman, illustrated by Charles Keeping: B L Kearley Ltd
Ways with Plays by Jackie Taylor, Mark Freeman & Jenny Bailey: Devon County Council,
The Angel of Nitshill Road by Anne Fine, illustrated by Kate Aldous: Egmont Children's Books Ltd
The Sandal by Tony Bradman, illustrated by Philippe Dupasquier: Anderson Press
Yanomami published by WWF-UK, Learning Through Action and Survival International
Letters from Heaven by Rachel Anderson, illustrated by Tony Kerins: Egmont Children's Books Ltd
A Picture 'And When Did You Last See Your Father?' by William Yeames: National Museums and Galleries on Merseyside
Anne Frank: Archive Photos/Archive Film, New York, USA
Back in the Playground Blues: reproduced by kind permission of Allison & Busby, London
An Extract from *The Diary of Anne Frank*: Penguin UK

We are grateful to the following for permissions to reproduce text:

Yanomami published by WWF-UK, Learning Through Action and Survival International
Article: Tough New Code to put Muzzle on 'Devil Dogs', Daily Mail 27 June 1990: Atlantic Syndication Partners
This Letter's to Say - Poem by the late Professor Raymond Wilson: Mrs G M Wilson

 2001
Published by NATE, 50 Broadfield Road,
Sheffield, S8 0XJ
Tel: 0114 255 5419
Fax: 0114 255 5296

ISBN 0 901291 79 X

Designed, typeset and printed by
Quorn Selective Repro Limited, Loughborough, Leicestershire.

CONTENTS

Page

feeling
and
sharing

Introduction

Everyone moved forward one at a time, to kneel beside the small cairn of rocks which covered the body of the young girl who has died. They whispered their farewells and left a precious token of remembrance.

> *'Louisa, this is my blood.'*
> *'This the rope you cut in half.'*
> *'Here's the picture of you and me together.'*
> *'Here's my precious stone,'*

Then the small party of pioneers, struggling to reach their promised land beyond the great Rockies of North America, turned their backs on her grave, and headed on into the snow covered mountains, leaving her as a memory of their past life and as a price for the new.

This improvisation was part of a drama which a class created about people's visions and the trials and tribulations they are prepared to face in order to achieve them. It was set within the context of the great migration West, around the middle of the nineteenth century, which as a historical narrative, reflects one of that century's many movements of people around the world. It is a testament to mankind's fortitude in the face of great odds, for it symbolises what can be endured and overcome, but also the price that is paid. Themes like these can be explored and reflected upon in drama, as imaginative echoes of the times and tides of other 'worlds'.

Such classroom drama is imaginatively and intellectually demanding; it involves making and shaping new worlds, and investigating issues in them. In this book we focus throughout on such drama, rather than on theatre or performance skills. Since although these are closely related to whole class improvisational drama, our explicit intention is to profile classroom drama and to provide teachers with a better grasp of it in practice. The pressures of recent years have reduced opportunities for creative activity in education, but children need such experiences to develop their imagination in action and to harness the potential of drama as a learning medium. In classroom drama, learners create and experience a living narrative and examine it from within. Their teacher, often in role, accompanies the class on this journey and uses a range of other drama conventions to investigate the themes, characters, motives or issues in the evolving tale. Reflecting upon these themes and finding parallels in real life is a significant part of the drama and heightens its relevance to the children.

This book is written for classroom teachers in primary schools, and English teachers in secondary schools who are not often drama specialists. Drama is an art form in its own right, and includes the integrated processes of making, performing and responding which become slightly more separated in the secondary years. In the secondary school, there may well be a drama department and the opportunity for children to undertake exam work, in which their performance ability will be developed, alongside their technical knowledge of the subject. But elements of performance are already integrated into classroom drama, in all activities which involve being watched by others, however momentarily. Making and responding to drama is also fully incorporated into classroom drama, which enables teachers to fulfil the statutory orders of the National Curriculum (1999) and develop children's imaginative and creative capacity.

We aim to support non-specialist teachers in planning and resourcing classroom drama, so in Part One a range of lessons, all of which have been taught and developed in classrooms, are offered. We hope teachers will make use of these example lessons and gradually become more confident in planning their own work and selecting appropriate resources to prompt dramatic investigations. There are a wide range of resources which can prompt classroom drama, including fiction and poetry, music and art, faith tales and history, science and geography, and the personal and social issues of the children's own lives, as well as themes such as citizenship. We've tried to reflect this diversity in the resource chapters and to show how drama can be integrated into cross-curricular work and operate as an effective learning strategy. The resources used here were chosen because they are potentially powerful, extremely engaging, and open to a variety of improvisational responses.

Whilst this book does not offer a sequential programme of drama sessions, the resource chapters do reflect a gradual increase in complexity and demand. The sessions are offered as stepping stones to increase confidence and competence in classroom drama, and as jumping - off points and resource banks for planning future dramas. Each of the resource chapters identifies the teaching objectives and learning areas, and provides a guiding framework for drama which involves: First Encounters: Creating the Drama Context, Conflicts and Tensions: Opening the Drama Out, and Resolutions: Drawing the Drama Together. Extension activities and ideas for resourcing further dramas from the named resources are also offered.

Several of the dramas described could be spread over a number of sessions, since if the children's initial encounter with the theme really hooks their interest, they will happily revisit the same drama with enthusiasm and commitment. This can extend their learning considerably through a more in-depth examination of the issues, which avoids simple stereotypes and examines a variety of perspectives. Do be selective in deciding upon the suggestions you wish to use from each chapter, much will depend upon the children's responses and interests, their experience of drama and the time available. Avoiding the children's suggestions and responses in order to follow the plan may mean that real opportunities for relevant learning are missed. So a professional balance between following the teaching objectives and the children's interests is always required.

In Part Two, issues around organising, teaching and assessing classroom drama are discussed. *Planning* classroom drama is examined in some detail to support the teacher in identifying the key elements of drama: people, place and predicament, which create a secure structure for the session. *Assessing* classroom drama is addressed, through considering the major areas of learning in drama, including, the imagination, personal and social skills, the drama process, language, reflection and the content area of the drama. All of the objectives extend those in our sister book, ***Resourcing Drama 5-8***. *Managing* the drama session is also considered and issues about control, noise and discipline are discussed alongside other concerns we've been asked about repeatedly. Since drama is placed within English in the National Curriculum for England and Wales, we have devoted one short chapter to *Drama and English*, noting how drama conventions can be harnessed in English time for developing inference in action in shared reading and as a powerful precursor to shared writing. However, we argue that merely employing a single drama convention for literacy purposes is not doing classroom drama full justice, since a range of conventions are required to fully investigate issues in texts and co-author new and living fictions. A couple of drama conventions are focused upon in each chapter and are examined further in the last chapter on *Drama Conventions* which seeks to explain the nature and function of the different conventions. In particular, teacher in role and teacher using narration are highlighted as strategies we recommend from the outset of teaching classroom drama.

Classroom drama represents much more than a way of responding to the statutory orders for English. It offers children the chance to create and inhabit imaginary worlds together and learn from living in drama time with their teacher. It has the potential to develop children's personal and social skills, their sense of identity, confidence and competence with language and their understanding of citizenship in the twenty-first century. It is a motivating and engaging process, a refreshing and empowering act of creativity.

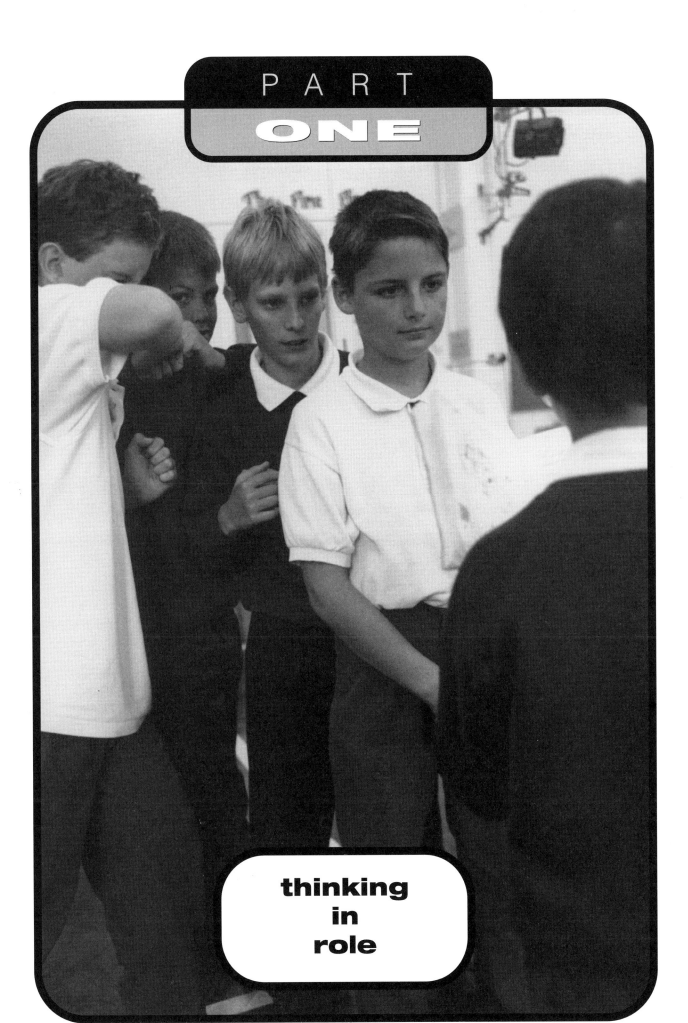

PART

ONE

thinking
in
role

Chapter 1

A PICTURE BOOK:
BLODIN THE BEAST BY MICHAEL MORPURGO

Introduction

This drama is based upon the issues and themes explored in the picture book *Blodin the Beast* by Michael Morpurgo (1995, Frances Lincoln). The story, fabulously illustrated by Christina Balit, is used in this drama to provide a framework for the imaginative investigation. The tale is read in sections and the visual images are shared in order to identify gaps in the text, which are developed, embellished and examined in the drama. So throughout, the narrative frames the drama, and the illustrations provide a creative space that the children can inhabit. The strength of the illustrations and the analogies offered in the tale make this picture book a valuable resource for drama.

The tale tells of how Blodin the Beast, a great creature of iron, enslaves whole villages, gradually forcing all the people in the land to dig oil for him. Soon there is just one village left, hidden deep in a mountain valley and inevitably Blodin seeks it out. The villagers have heard rumours of the Beast and decide to bow before him, but wise old Shanga, their leader, refuses to do so. 'I will be no-one's slave' he argues and continues to weave his life's work, a precious carpet. The carpet has particular significance and becomes a tool used by young Hosea to end Blodin's rule. So it is through faith, the wisdom of age and the courage of youth that Blodin is finally defeated.

The convention of **teacher in role** is highlighted in this chapter. This involves the teacher in adopting different roles to extend and challenge the children's appreciation of various perspectives. Also **group sculpture** is used to summarise the issues examined by the text. This convention prompts the children to discuss their own individual interpretation of the events and come to some agreement in order to create an abstract piece of sculpture.

Avoiding the children's suggestions and responses in order to follow the plan may mean that real opportunities for relevant leaning are missed. A professional balance between teaching objectives and children's interests is always required.

Teaching Objectives and Learning Areas

- Contribute ideas in the imaginary situation (*the imagination*).
- Co-operate thoughtfully in small group and whole class work (*personal and social skills*).
- Recognise and name a range of drama conventions (*the drama process*).

Prior Experience and Materials

No experience is necessary, although the drama would fit well in a history focus on the industrial revolution, since Blodin also represents industrialisation and the villagers' responses can be seen to reflect the pressure, fear and conformity which accompanied it.

- Photocopies of the book jacket (with the title blanked out), the inside cover, and the first double page spread
- Photocopies of Hosea's dream (p.9 with the writing removed from the smoke bubble)
- Large pieces of paper, pencils and crayons.

First Encounters: Creating the Drama Context

FEARS AND RUMOURS ABOUND

- Divide the class into groups of four and give each group a photocopy of the front cover of the text (having blanked out the title). Explain this is a book cover, and ask them to talk about what they can see and generate ideas from this.
- Pass each group a photocopy of the inside cover that shows Hosea and Shanga. Ask them to discuss how this illustration of two unknown characters from the story adds to their understanding and predictions about the tale. Let them share some of their thoughts and reflect on the source of these.

- Pass each group a photocopy of the first double page spread and read the text aloud to the class in a foreboding tone, '*Blodin the Beast stalked the land, he drank only oil, he breathed only fire*' ... and so on until the end of this page.
- Suggest to the class that rumours and gossip about the Beast abound and that in one untouched village, high in the mountains, people shared the stories they'd heard. Suggest that some were true, some exaggerated, some quite incredible, but all the tales passed on about Blodin the Beast struck fear into the hearts of those who heard them. Ask the children, in pairs, to make up a rumour or a short story about Blodin's exploits, which they can retell. Circulate informally listening to their ideas.
- Join pairs together to make groups of four, and, in a storyteller's voice, inform them that at sunset that day, many people gathered in the market square to share the tales they'd heard. Ask each pair to retell the tale they had previously created together, and listen to snippets of these.

Conflicts and Tensions: Developing the Drama

A STRANGER AMONGST US

- Allow time for their tales to be told, but while they are still retelling in pairs, arrive in role as a slave who has escaped from Blodin's clutches, and prompt a whole class improvisation by asking for food, drink and comfort. Tell them you believe Blodin is coming this way, what will they do, can they hide you? During this improvisation, tell them you have worked for him, but as you've escaped with insider's knowledge of the Beast, you will tell them what they need to know, if they'll only help you. Respond in kind to their words and actions, e.g. if they are suspicious of you, then perhaps you will reveal little, but if they treat you well, tell them what you know. You can use the ideas shared in their stories.

- As storyteller, retell the events which unfold in this whole class improvisation and reflect upon the attitudes of the villagers, you could suggest that some were less than sure of him, which will add tension if they have been entirely welcoming. Then, move the story on and suggest that when the villagers retired to bed that night, their dreams turned to nightmares as they saw before them Blodin's land of slaves, oppressed and afraid, forced to obey his will.

- Ask the children in small groups to create a freeze-frame of this land of servitude, the foreboding image which the people saw in their dreams. Is Blodin really omnipotent…?

- As these are being prepared, visit each group and ask the children to add voices or a repetitive ritual chant to their nightmare. As a class, observe each of these premonitions of the future, reflecting upon the ways the meanings have been conveyed.

WHY WILL SHANGA NOT COME WITH US?

- Read, or preferably narrate, the second page and only the first paragraph of the third page of the book. In this, the villagers feel the earth shake, and full of fear, agree to go and bow before Blodin to save themselves. However, Shanga, the oldest and wisest amongst them, refuses to leave, he wishes to complete his life's work which is a woven carpet.

- Paint a word picture of Shanga, their revered leader, shaman and friend, and reflect on how the villagers feel, voicing some memories on their behalf. For example, some recalled how he had cured diseases and laid on healing hands, others how he had offered wise counsel in their disputes and led them succesfully. Many wondered why he refused to lead them now in their hour of need. Explain that the villagers come to say their goodbyes, believing they must persuade him to come with them or else he'll perish.

- Suggest the children discuss in 2/3's what the villagers might say to Shanga to persuade him to submit to Blodin, and if he refuses, how will they say goodbye and thank him for his leadership? Allow the children time to discuss what they might say to Shanga.

- As narrator, describe how the villagers gathered together at the mouth of the cave where Shanga sat weaving, many questioned his decision to stay, others thanked him and said goodbye.

(8-year-olds)

- Tell the class you are going into role as Shanga and then respond to their questions with dignity and care. In your replies highlight the significance of your carpet and hint at the pictures of life portrayed within it. You know many truths and do not believe good will overcome evil, so you are not afraid of Blodin. Remain resolute in your decision to remain in your cave and complete your carpet, and suggest the villagers leave to submit to Blodin or they will anger him. This should prompt them to say their goodbyes.

- Read/Tell the rest of page 3 in which young Hosea, who has no parents, begs to stay with Shanga, who agrees and tells him 'There is more than wool in this carpet my son.'

- Ask the children in small groups to discuss why the carpet is precious and to make a picture of it, its many pictures, symbols, patterns and shapes. Provide large pieces of paper and pencils/crayons and give time to complete these. Then, as a class, examine each one and ask the group to explain the understanding they've reached about the significance of the carpet.

HOSEA'S TRAVELS

- Read or narrate the next two pages of the tale, when Hosea is directed by Shanga to take the finished carpet and escape over the mountains, Shanga promises the carpet will guide and protect him, as he travels in search of a land of peace and plenty. Hosea sets off into the mountains alone, knowing he will be tested many times and that Blodin will surely search him out.

- Ask the children in small groups to improvise one of Hosea's trials, reminding them of their carpet drawings and previous ideas. When they are ready, link their group improvisations together through your narration, describing what you have just seen and then introducing the next improvised trial.

Hayley (aged 8)

- As Hosea, either individually or in pairs, write a letter to Shanga or a diary entry describing one of the trials he had to face.

- Tell or read the next section of the tale in which Hosea travels through mountains, jungles and across the desert (each are given a double page spread) and how at night he sleeps wrapped safely in the precious carpet. Inform the class that Hosea's dreams of the meeting between old Shanga and Blodin the Beast, the forces of good and evil, but do not read beyond page 8, where he is in the desert.

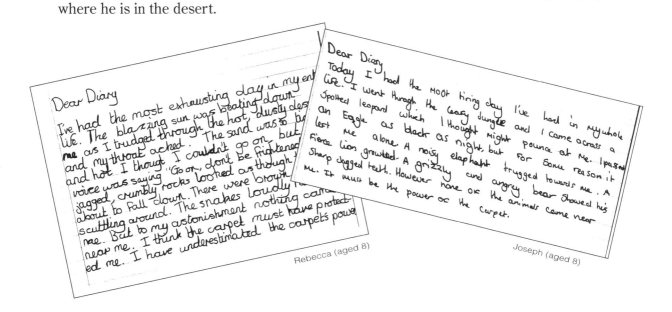

Dear Diary
I've had the most exhausting day in my entire life. The blazing sun was beating down on me as I trudged through the hot, dusty desert and my throat ached. The sand was so hot. I thought I couldn't go on, but a voice was saying "Go on, don't be frightened." Jagged, crumbly rocks looked as though they were about to fall down. There were brown snakes scuttling around. The snakes loudly hissed near me. But to my astonishment nothing came near me. I think the carpet must have protected me. I have underestimated the carpet's power.

Rebecca (aged 8)

Dear Diary
Today I had the most tiring day I've had in my whole life. I went through the scary jungle and I came across a spotted leopard which I thought might pounce at me. I passed an Eagle as black as night, but for some reason it let me alone. A noisy elephant trudged towards me. A fierce lion growled. A grizzly and angry bear showed his sharp jagged teeth. However none of the animals came near me. It must be the power of the carpet.

Joseph (aged 8)

'I WILL BE NO ONE'S SLAVE'

- Divide the class into two, half to represent Shanga, half to represent Blodin, and create a space between the two groups to show where Hosea lay dreaming. Give time for the children to discuss what Shanga and the Beast might say to one another. Give out photocopies of the double page spread of the dream (with the writing removed). Offer a few possibilities to prompt their thinking; will Shanga reveal

Hosea has escaped from Blodin's clutches? Will he tell Blodin he can never win, or will he seek to understand the Beast's actions? Indeed will Blodin want to know why Shanga will not submit to him, does he think Shanga is just an old fool? Surely Shanga knows that Blodin is the most powerful creature on the earth?

- Before you begin this improvised confrontation, make it clear each side must listen and respond to each other, and not talk at once. You could insist on Shanga and Blodin taking turns if you think the class need this structure. Sit down with Shanga's group and start the conversation asking why Blodin has come, does he wish to take over the world, can it not be shared? Work with the class at this argumentative debate examining issues of power, greed, faith and perceived foolishness. Critical issues include what Blodin seeks to gain, and why Shanga should have waited for his death, why will he not submit, are there forces stronger than both of them at work? In essence, this is a debate between good and evil.

- When the debate has reached its natural conclusion, read the words on page 9 in which Morpurgo describes Shanga's conversation with Blodin and the old man's death. Draw the class together and reflect on the points raised by both the text and the class's representation of this meeting.

Resolutions: Drawing the Drama Together

LEARNING FROM THE PAST

- With the children still around you read the rest of the story to them.

- Ask the children to create small group sculptures that sum up the truth about the tale and to title their sculpture accordingly. Suggest these are abstract non-representational sculptures, so the characters in the tale will not be present, but the qualities they represent can be shown. As a class observe each piece, reflecting together upon them. Discuss what evidence each group used to come to their conclusions.

- List the title of their sculptures on a flipchart and discuss any connections or parallels in their lives, in history or in other texts or contexts, as well as considering the embodiment of good and evil which are represented in the story and/or the theme of industrialisation.

Extension Activities

- Re-examine Blodin the Beast within a literacy focus. The story structure could be reconstructed as a class map to aid retelling, the dream photocopy could be used to capture Shanga's last conversation in writing or further diary entries could be made. Extracts from the text could also be focused upon to highlight one of the character's behaviour, appearance, emotions or speech.

- Ask the class to collect and display parallel tales or other texts (eg. newspaper articles) which also explore the identified themes, or have key characters that personify good and evil.

- Use the carpet drawings as the basis for artwork. Now that the story has unfolded are there elements the children would like to develop or change?

Resourcing Further Drama from Picture Books

Challenging picture books represent rich resources for dramatic investigation, as they contain strong predicaments and often very high quality illustrations that draw the learners into the imaginative world of the text. The complex themes in these multimodal texts can be woven into the drama, and the visual images offered in them can be used in the drama in a variety of ways, either in harmony with the written text or in contrast to the words. Possible ways of using such texts are noted on pages 13–14.

1   Taking the Book as a Guide

Read or tell the first part of the tale, and share the pictures, stopping intermittently to allow the children to examine the gaps left by the text, eg. what the characters were thinking, who else did they talk to? Then read or tell the next part of the story, and flesh out more of the unwritten text through drama before returning again to the tale. Continue in this manner to the end. In this way the tale works to guide the drama, but re-enactment is not sought. Instead the class travel alongside the tale, improvising the gaps and expanding the meanings. It is also possible to start by letting the text guide the drama and then to leave the narrative behind during the dramatic investigation, allowing the children's ideas to shape the unfolding drama. The text can be read later for a comparison. We recommend the following.

Sleeping Nannah (1989), Kevin Crossley Holland, illus. by Peter Melnyczuk, Orchard.
Nannah goes to 'sleep' and travels the ocean visiting the five islands of the senses. This offers plenty of scope for being guided by the text structure, exploring each island in turn and responding to invented challenges on each.

The Tunnel (1989), Anthony Browne, Julia MacRae.
Difficult sibling relationships are examined in this text in which the brother disappears through a tunnel into another world. He can only be rescued from this metaphorical world by his sister. It is good for decision alley work, thought tracking and exploring gender issues.

Going West (1983), Martin Waddell, illus. by Philippe Dupasquier, Picture Puffin.
A family of American pioneers take the wagon train West and find their journey is packed with challenges. Written in the first person as a journal, this book prompts writing in role and is very suitable as a guide for drama.

2   Creating their own Tale from an Opening Scenario

Read, tell or show pictures from only the first part of a tale and then move into drama mode and improvise the remainder of the text, examining previous and future action, as well as character behaviour and motives and the themes being explored. A range of drama conventions would be employed to achieve this. The author's tale can be read to the class when they've created their own story through drama. We recommend the following.

I'll take you to Mrs Cole (1985), Nigel Gray, illus. by Michael Foreman, Picture Mac.
In this story, fear of the unknown is examined, challenged and resolved. Through drama the children may solve the 'mystery' of Mrs Cole in other ways and co-author their own alternative version of the tale.

Shaker Lane (1987), Alice and Martin Provensen, Walker Books.
The rural community of Shaker Lane lives happily together, but are faced with change when their land is summarily purchased and swift urbanisation follows. Building the sense of community and then threatening its existence, creates a powerful context for drama and lets the class find its own solutions.

The Boy and The Cloth of Dreams (1994) Jenny Koralek, illus. by James Matthew, Walker
This text describes a young boy's visit to his grandmother's house, with his torn cloth of dreams. He forgets to ask her to mend it and is therefore subjected to terrible nightmares and has to learn to forge his own courage and independence. The powerful illustrations offer several leaping off points for drama.

3   Creating a Follow Up Text

Read or tell the complete tale and then create a drama that is built on its shoulders, either as a parallel tale or by taking the same characters into another predicament and exploring their responses and the issues which emerge. Again the drama needs to dig down into the themes, and behaviour, motives and attitudes of these characters. An earlier tale can also be created through dramatic exploration. We recommend the following.

Voices in the Park (1988), Anthony Browne, Doubleday.
A revisited version of Browne's earlier *A Walk in the Park*, in which we meet four people who all visit the park and through their own inner voices and the powerful illustrations we perceive four different perspectives. The lives of another four people who visit the park could be created and their motivations and interests examined in more detail, or the lives of the same two families could be fleshed out in other contexts to create a follow up tale.

Way Home (1994) Libby Hathorn, illus. by Gregory Rogers, Andersen.
Shane, a homeless youngster finds a stray cat in the city. He protects it and takes it to his cardboard 'home'. A follow up drama can examine the challenges which Shane experiences as a homeless youngster in a big city, or investigate how he came to be living there in the first place.

The Watertower (1994) Gary Grew, illus. by Steven Woolman, Era.
This mysterious and somewhat sinister tale recounts the emanating influence of the water tower through two boys, Spike and Bubba. Is the town hypnotised by it, in a trance - like state? There are simply no answers only possibilities, which makes it a great book to follow up in drama. What happens when a new family moves in?

4   Prefiguring the Text through Drama

Identify the theme and issues in the picture book and develop a drama around these prior to reading the book to the class. You may choose to offer the children the title of the text or simply not to mention the book. In effect the drama investigation is an analogy for the text, which on some occasions will be closely allied to the known narrative and the characters, while on others will only be connected to the text through its themes. In the latter example, the people and the place may well be very different, but the essential predicament and the theme, for example, of disappointment and disillusionment will be prefigured and examined through the drama. Almost any text can be used in this way, we recommend the following.

Window (1991), Jeannie Baker, Red Fox.
This wordless picture book examines the changing face of the world. The issue of environmental destruction can be explored through one community's response, with role play, hot seating, marches, community meetings and so forth, which bring to life the human cost of urbanisation.

Sammy Streetsinger (1984) Charles Keeping, Oxford
This tale chart Sammy's rise to fame in the world of pop music, but his stardom is short lived and empty since he is alone. Exploring through drama an individual/group's journey to fame and fortune, and the challenges and identity conflicts involved makes an interesting precursor to the text.

Why (1996), Nikolai Popov, North - South Books.
A wordless picture book which explores the origins and consequences of aggression. While the pictures depict frogs and mice, parallel contexts are easily identifiable on the playground, at home, in the community and the wider world. The escalating cycle of violence and the senselessness of war can be actively explored through drama that explores the issues in another context.

Chapter 2
A LETTER: CREATING A LOCAL MUSEUM

> *TONBRIDGE COUNCIL*
> *The Mayor's Parlour,*
> *The Council Offices,*
> *The Ridgeway*
>
> *Mon 6th June 2000*
>
> *Dear   ,*
>
> *I am writing to you on behalf of the Mayor of Tonbridge. You are someone whose work in this town has been brought to our notice, indeed your commitment to this town is held in the highest regard. So the Mayor and all the councillors would value your opinion on a rather unusual and exciting new venture.*
>
> *The town has recently received a large sum of money for the establishment of our own Museum. The generous benefactor wishes to remain anonymous, but has made it a condition of the offer that the people of the town should decide what the Museum should focus upon. It is with this in mind that you are invited to come to a meeting at the Council offices on Tuesday 15th July at 9:30 am to suggest ideas for the Museum. Please discuss the matter with your family, friends and neighbours, so that as many people's views as possible are represented. I trust you are able to join the Mayor and look forward to seeing you then.*
>
> *Yours sincerely,*
>
> *Melissa Brown*
> *Deputy Mayor.*

Introduction

This drama uses a letter of invitation as a hook, to prompt the children's imaginative engagement, and to cast the children as members of the town whose advice has been sought to create a new museum. We refer to a town as the site of the drama, but it could equally well be a village or rural area with appropriate adjustments. Letters are a useful resource in drama as they set a fictional frame, provide contextual information and can sow seeds of potential conflict. They also offer a degree of authenticity to the enterprise, particularly if they are delivered, addressed and stamped.

In this drama, the letter arrives to inform the class that an anonymous benefactor has donated considerable capital to create a museum, but is determined that it must reflect the lives and interests of the community in some way. Since the drama is therefore based upon the children's own views, choices and their town, they find it very appealing. They work together in small groups and as a whole class planning, designing and stocking their museum. The focus of the museum can be any area of the curriculum although they will also find out about the lives and motivations of ordinary people. In making democratic decisions about their museum the children, in the role of active citizens, will be exploring their knowledge of the community and other aspects of citizenship education.

The conventions highlighted in this drama are **small group improvisation,** both planned and spontaneous and **playmaking**. Spontaneous improvisation is quite demanding since it requires children to listen and respond rapidly and appropriately. Small group playmaking by contrast, allows for planning, practice and presentation, even if the eventual improvisation is extremely short. Encouraging children to respond to each other's play-lets is also integrated into this drama, creating an opportunity for some forum theatre. This enables the chosen improvisation to be revisited using several of the ideas suggested by the class.

Avoiding the children's suggestions and responses in order to follow the plan may mean that real opportunities for relevant learning are missed. A professional balance between teaching objectives and children's interests is always required.

Teaching Objectives and Learning Areas

- Visualise and articulate clear ideas in the drama (*the imagination*).
- Use language to make a reasoned argument, to debate and persuade others of their point of view (*language*).
- Consider different citizens' perspectives, and develop their understanding of the focus of the museum (*the content of the drama*).

Prior Experience and Materials

No prior experience is necessary, although this would fit well within a focus on local history or work on the local area. The children will be explicitly using their knowledge of exhibitions; displays and interactive museums so planning the drama to follow a museum trip would be advantageous.

- Copies of the letter for each member of the class inside one large envelope.
- Large sheets of paper and pencils.
- Eight blank postcards or similarly sized card.

First Encounters: Creating the Drama Context

THE INVITATIONS

- Tell the class that later that day you're all going to do a drama about making a museum for your area or town. Discuss with the class the various kinds of people who might be invited to an initial meeting. List these on the board and ensure a cross section of society is invited. Discuss their favourite museums and the reasons for their preferences. Allow a reasonable amount of time between this forewarning and the actual arrival of the letters, as this will help build interest and engagement.
- Arrange for the secretary to deliver the invitations, sealed in an envelope. Hand these out and allow time for reading.

THE FIRST PLANNING MEETING

- Ask the class to visualise the Council Chamber where the meeting is to be held, and then ask them what they see: the carpet, the furniture, and the walls, portraits, flowers, display cabinets and so on.
- Using the children's suggestions rearrange the classroom to represent the Council Chamber and while they're doing this, ask them each to choose one of the listed roles. Prompt them to consider the following biographical details of their roles: name, occupation, age, and information about their family.

- Revisit the list on the board, which should give the children time to complete the details in their head, and ask them to take a seat in the Council Chamber when they are ready.
- Inform the class you're going to join the meeting shortly, and walk away from them, saying that when you turn round, you'll be someone else. Pause perceptibly, listen for quiet and then join the meeting as the Deputy Mayor. Welcome them formally, apologise for the Mayor's absence and outline the project. Money has been donated to the local council for a new museum and they've been invited to express their views and ideas about what kind of theme/s the museum might adopt and how the money might be spent.

- Prompt the children to enter this whole class improvisation by asking for their opinions and ask each speaker to introduce him or herself and include some information about their work and position in the town.
- As chair of the meeting, push the children to detail their ideas, invite other views and consider alternatives. Possible themes might include toys, music, fashion, leisure, food, science, childhood family life, and so on, the list is endless. Practical issues also need to be considered; do they wish for a café, gift shop, interactive displays or static exhibits? If suggestions are made to spend the money on other things, eg. a new football pitch, make it clear the benefactor has stipulated a museum.
- Close the meeting formally and stress the value of the many ideas posed. Invite them all to a follow up meeting, when groups can present more detailed proposals and a final decision will be taken.

Conflicts and Tensions: Developing the Drama

ALTERNATIVE PLANS AND PROPOSALS
- Through shared writing produce a brief local newspaper report about the forthcoming museum and the ideas suggested so far. This might include locals' views and should raise the question of the purpose of the museum and whose interests it should reflect. In effect this writing will reflect the earlier discussion but needs to raise questions about the museum.
- In small groups of four/five ask the children to agree a theme for the museum and design the ground floor space. Hand out large sheets of paper and plenty of pencils. Encourage them to produce detailed plans of the rooms, bays and sections, showing the displays, events and items in them. Allow time for groups to consolidate their ideas and increase the commitment to their plan.
- Ask groups to agree which members will present their proposal at the meeting and to identify what they will say to persuade others that their idea is the best.

THE SECOND PLANNING MEETING
- In a whole class improvisation, with you in the role as Deputy Mayor again, create the second planning meeting and invite each group to persuade the meeting to adopt their idea. Only allow a brief presentation time per group, but do encourage questions and comments. Work towards agreeing a focus, your class may choose one single theme or may prefer to reflect

the diversity in the area and in effect allow each group a room. Either way there will undoubtedly be gaps and groups in the wider community whose interests are not reflected in the museum. Be sure to voice your concerns about this and debate these issues at the meeting. It is difficult to please everyone.

- Suggest to the class that when the final decision about the museum went public and press releases described the plan, several pressure groups and individual members of the public were dissatisfied and voiced their views in letters to the local paper.

- Ask children to pair up and write either a letter of complaint about the museum justifying their views, or an article by the management committee seeking to persuade the public that their choice is sound. These will need to include a series of arguments, and might comment upon the process of decision making and involvement of local citizens.

SELECTING EXHIBITS

- Ask each planning group to suggest one object, which has been donated to the museum, and suits the chosen theme(s), and sculpt it with their bodies. This piece of group sculpture could be a moving or a static exhibit. Once these are created, don't observe them as a class but move quickly on.

- Ask the groups to compose the descriptive paragraph, which accompanies this object. This should include exactly what it is, what it's made of, who donated it and why it has been included. Hand out blank postcards for this purpose.

- As a class, observe each exhibit in turn and listen to the supporting resumé about each one, pondering with the children on why the donors gave these objects, and what significance it might have for them.

Pokémon Cards

This set of cards was collected by Matthew Evans, while he was at The Slade School, Tonbridge. He was a pupil there between 1994-2000. The cards were highly prized by the pupils and this collection is particularly note-worthy because it is complete. The cards were produced by Leisure Products International (UK) LTD under licence to Nintendo Corp.

Matthew Evans, of Bordyke Rd, Tonbridge, donated the cards.

Matthew (aged 9)

Iron Horse Shoe

This shoe was found beneath the walls of Tonbridge Castle by workmen digging out the Tunnels in 1985. It was believed the owners of the Red Lion Hotel in the High Street used the Tunnels as stables for many years. There are stories that smugglers, (in the 18th century), from Romney, used the tunnels on their way up to London with brandy from France.

The shoe was donated by Mrs Caroline Monks of Downs Way Stables, Hadlow.

Lisa (aged 9)

Model of the Crane at Berth 4, Chatham Royal Naval Dock yard

The apprentices in the metal yard at the dockyard made this model in 1940. The crane was used to lift heavy equipment such as boilers and heavy armaments like the 14 INS guns, in and out of warships. It was constructed in 1921 and taken out of use in 1959 to make way for the present hydraulic ramps. The model is fully working and is powered by the steam boiler alongside it.

The model was donated in memory of Mr Alfred King of Sheldon Road, Tonbridge. Mr King worked at the dockyard between 1940-1980, first as an apprentice, and finally as yard manager. His family have lived in the area since 1911.

Adam (aged 9)

THE LOCAL PEOPLE

- Explain to the class, that the museum could not have existed without the community who shaped it through their debates in the Council meetings and in the local press. The donors of the objects too have given of themselves. You want to explore some of the people behind the museum, their lives and families. Ask each group to select one family who was involved (as supporters, organisers, objectors or donors) and prepare a brief play-let about them. This could involve their views about the museum, or the object (if they've donated one), but must show something about a conflict or difficulty in their lives and their views of the museum.

- Move around the groups, assisting with ideas and stressing the relative brevity of this play-let, select one group to use for forum theatre later. This needs to be a group capable of taking advice and ideas from their classmates.

- Observe each of these brief play-lets, leaving the selected one until last, (or agree with the class, other occasions when some can be shared). Prompt the class to discuss the improvisations watched, focusing on the views shown about the museum, and each group's ability to communicate the different characters and the relationships between them.

Resolutions: Drawing the Drama Together

PEOPLE'S PERSPECTIVES

- Explain to the children before the last play-let is shown that you are going to use this one for forum theatre. This means that when you (or they) clap to stop the action, the rest of the class can offer advice to the characters, suggest a course of action and comment upon the scene. This will then be revisited, and the characters will try to use the ideas given.

- Watch the chosen improvisation and when the action is stopped, ask the individual characters to join a small group of classmates, who should offer advice and ideas to that person. Then continue the scene, extending it, or restarting it to highlight the family's perception of the museum.

- Discuss together what all these play-lets tell you about the people in the community. Highlight the differences and similarities between them and in particular their various views about the museum, and their involvement in the venture. Ponder on whether everyone in the town was represented, and whether there was a fair representation of views.

- Consider how diverse perspectives are voiced in society, through the media and in democratic institutions such as local councils, pressure groups and voluntary bodies. Discuss whether any of the class are members of clubs or associations, eg.: Scouts, St John's Ambulance, Youth Club, RSPCA, Greenpeace, etc. and how decisions are made in these organisations.

Extension Activities

- Produce promotional pamphlets advertising the museum with its mission statement, include information, special events and diagrams of the interior.

- Create a guidebook for the museum with entries from each group on their area, the designs, exhibits, resumés and so on.

- Link this work to design and technology and humanities and/or a citizenship focus.

- Extend the drama further by focusing on one of the objects and its possibly chequered history as a possession.

Resourcing Further Drama from Letters

Letters are effective and diverse resources for drama, because they often pass on information, describe feelings or events, and represent unfinished material. This open-endedness enables the class to build on the clues and information offered to construct their drama, and explore the themes and events suggested in the letter. Authenticity is an influential factor and it is worth spending time creating appropriate letters. Letters can encourage ownership of the direction of the drama and enable the children to make collective choices about their focus. Letters can also be found during drama, to create tension or provide information about a character, eg. the museum workers might be sent a letter stating that the museum should never be allowed to open, or that a significant object was donated in error and its return is requested. The suggestions below however focus on using letters to initiate drama.

1   Letters from Known Characters

Letters can be written from a variety of characters, somewhat in the style of Allan Ahlberg's *The Jolly Postman*. Such letters offer entry into known texts and tend to work best with lower KS2 learners. For example, the Director of Wonderment Films in *The Dancing Bear* by Michael Morpurgo, could write to invite the class to become members of the film crew. Or Tim, the less than confident hero in Jacqueline Wilson's *Cliffhanger* could invite the class to join him on his adventure holiday. Such letters enable the children to create new chapters in the text and afterwards compare these with the author's version.

2   Letters which bestow Expertise and a Role

Letters can be invented to relate to cross curricular work and used to give the children clear roles, an area of expertise, and a focus to work upon. For example, letters inviting esteemed archaeologists to join Howard Carter on his trip to excavate the Egyptian Valley of the Kings, or letters inviting scientists to a Conservation Conference to plan a national environmental drive. Equally letters of information, rather than invitation can be composed by the teacher to suit a drama. For example, letters to the police force from HQ providing scant information about a crime or a missing child. The class can then work to collect evidence and solve the mystery.

3   Genuine Pamphlets which provide Contextual Information

Real promotional materials from a theme park, zoo, caves, ancient building or waterworld can be useful resources to start a drama session. Such publicity pamphlets are freely available, attractive and interesting and can help develop the sense of the place and motivate the children to construct a drama around it. This may involve an imaginary day trip to the theme park or might focus on the workers in the water-world or a local 12th century, National Trust property, and the challenges which beset them. Such drama is often able to be integrated into a cross-curricular focus and can be related to English work or persuasive writing.

4   Texts which are comprised of Letters

Letters can be found in many fiction texts. These can be read partially to the class, stopping at a letter which framesets a problem and starting the drama from there. Alternatively analogies can be created, for example the drama could focus on the school trip to an adventure centre and during it the class could write letters or postcards home. This would prefigure the later reading of Bernard Ashley's short story 'Dear Bren' in *I'm Trying to Tell You* (Puffin) as a parallel tale told in letters. We recommend the following, all of which are constructed as letters.

Anderson, Rachel (1996), *Letters from Heaven*, Mammoth
Anholt, Laurence (1995), *Magpie Song*, Heinemann.
Ashley, Bernard (1981), Dear Bren in *I'm Trying to Tell You*, Puffin

Croser, Josephine (1991), *Dear Sam, Dear Ben*, Era
Stewart, Sarah (1997), *The Gardener*, Collins
Townson, Hazel (1990), *Deathwood Letters*, Red Fox
Whybrow, Ian (1996), *Little Wolf's Book of Badness*, Collins
Wilson, Jacqueline (1995), *Cliffhanger*, Corgi (a tale with letters interspersed)
Yildrim, Elijay (1997), *Aunty Dot's Atlas*, Collins.

Letters in newspapers and magazines take many forms (eg. complaints, views, commentaries, problem page concerns and so on). All of these are potential resources for drama and can give access to political debates, personal and social issues and moral explorations. The authenticity of these encourages speculation and construction of the wider narrative in which the letter was written. Poems in the form of letters are also useful, as for example Raymond Wilson's *This Letter's to Say*, which, for example, provides scope to hold community meetings with the council, to voice views in written form, and to examine the consequences for local inhabitants and the environment.

This Letter's to Say

Dear Sir or Madam
This letter's to say
Your property
Stands bang in the way
Of Progress, and
Will be knocked down
On March the third
At half-past one.

There is no appeal,
Since the National Need
Depends on more And
still more Speed,
And this, in turn,
Dear Sir or Madam,
Depends on half England
Being tar-macadam.
(But your house will -
We are pleased to say -
Be the fastest lane
of the Motorway.)

Meanwhile the Borough
Corporation
Offer you new
Accommodation
Three miles away
On the thirteenth floor
(Flat Number Q 6824).

But please take note,
The Council regret:
No dog, cat, bird
Or other pet;
No noise permitted
No singing in the bath
(For permits to drink
Or smoke or laugh
Apply on form Z327);
No children admitted
Aged under eleven;
No hawkers; tramps
No roof-top lunches;
No opening doors
To Bible-punchers.

Failure to pay
Your rent, when due,
Will lead to our
Evicting you.
The Council demand
That you consent
To all terms above
When you pay your rent.

Meanwhile we hope
You will feel free
To consult us
Should there prove to be
The slightest case
Of difficulty.

With kind regards,
Yours faithfully...

Raymond Wilson

Tough new code to put muzzle on 'devil dogs'

FEROCIOUS dogs are to be brought to heel under a tough crackdown on problem pets.

Courts will be able to impose muzzling orders on animals regarded by neighbours, dog wardens or the police as likely to cause an injury – and owners may be ordered never to let their animals off the lead.

They will face heavy fines if they allow dangerous dogs to roam unsupervised. There will also be £10 fixed penalties for any of Britain's six million owners failing to provide a collar and tag.

The details are included in Government proposals, to be announced today, aimed at removing the fear spread by pets running out of control.

Owners who let their dogs on to the streets during working hours will risk a charge of up to £50 to collect pets picked up as strays, while persistent offenders could be fined £200.

But there will be no blanket ban on rottweilers, Staffordshire bull and English bull terriers – the breeds blamed for the most savage attacks on children. A Government review showed that alsatians caused most injuries, while numerous attacks involved trusted breeds.

As a result, there will be a new offence of allowing any dog to be 'dangerously out of control', and stronger powers for councils and police to seize and destroy potential killers. Junior Environment Minister

By SEAN RYAN
Environment Correspondent

David Heathcoat-Amory promised a package of 'simple, tough, direct measures targeting identified problems'.

The Government has rejected calls for a dog registration scheme, which the RSPCA claims is vital to prevent a growing number of attacks and strays.

Mrs Thatcher believes registration, to be pressed in the Lords next week as an amendment to the Green Bill would be expensive and ineffective.

Widow Mary Dolan, 79, from Bradley Road, Litherland, Liverpool, was recovering in hospital last night after being savagely attacked by a rottweiler which leaped over her garden fence. The dog was destroyed.

Devil dogs?

"The criticism that has been heaped on what the media have dubbed 'devil dogs' would be more rightly directed at the callous owners who neglect, brutalise and abuse these animals," said RSPCA Chief Officer of Inspectorate Richard Davies. Many people, he said are simply using large, powerful dogs as status symbols to enhance a macho image. They take them on with little thought or knowledge of the dog's welfare and then discard their new pet as a child would a new toy it was bored with.

Welfare crisis

The crisis in dog welfare, illustrated by Elsa, Suzy and the rest of the RSPCA's 1989 dog-cruelty statistics demonstrates the overwhelming need for a Government introduced, compulsory dog registration scheme, says Mr Davies.

"Registration would provide a framework for keeping track of irresponsible owners," he said. "Many people responsible for appalling abuse get off scot free either because we can't trace them or prove they are the owners."

In Suzy's case the irresponsible owners were easy to trace. They were in the flat when Inspector Jon Storey arrived. But Elsa was a different matter. She had been abandoned and wore no identifying mark to link her with an owner.

Described by a vet as the thinnest dog she had ever seen alive, this abandoned Rottweiler was found collapsed and in a pitiful state in a kitchen by a Brixton-based RSPCA Inspector. Not a scrap of food or water was in evidence; his owners had fled a week before. All attempts to locate them failed. Without a registration scheme, callous owners such as this are impossible to trace. The dog was destroyed despite valliant efforts to save him.

Dogs linked to owners

A dog registration scheme enforced by a national network of dog wardens, as suggested by the RSPCA, would mean however, that all dogs would be linked with their owners – responsible or irresponsible – through a permanent means of identification, either a tattoo or a microchip implant. This would mean that in cruelty cases, like Elsa's, the owner could be easily traced and held accountable for his or her actions.

Elsa the fully-grown rottweiler suffering from neglect and chronic starvation and weighing only 30 lbs, in the arms of her rescuer, RSPCA Inspector Tim Wass.

Chapter 3

A NEWSPAPER ARTICLE: DEVIL DOG ATTACKS CHILD!

Introduction

This drama sought to explore an item of current news in which the children expressed considerable interest. It evolved during a spate of dog attacks and the accompanying media debate about the dangers of trained guard dogs, such as Japanese Tozers, Staffordshire bull terriers and Rottweilers. Newspaper extracts at the time provided useful resources to heighten the sense of the tension and reflect the public fear about the mismanagement of these animals. Newspaper articles allow contemporary concerns to be examined, but in this particular drama they are used retrospectively to show the difficulties which led up to the introduction of dog licenses, muzzling and new laws about canines. The drama should help the class understand the complexity of the issue and the different representations of such issues in the media.

The drama explores a genuine incident in which a starving Rottweiler escaped and attacked a child on a school playground in Dartford. The children are given the headline of a national news report about the issue and are told of the attack. They then re-create the event and explore what led up to the attack and the consequences of it. In examining the facts, opinions, rumours and views held by various individuals, the drama offers the opportunity to examine different perspectives on the theme and create some of these in written form.

The drama conventions highlighted in this chapter are **hot seating**, **overheard conversations** and **writing in role**. Hot seating involves the teacher and/or members of the class in taking up particular roles and being questioned by the rest of the class who are also in role, in this case as newspaper reporters. This is a useful technique for highlighting different perspectives. Writing in role, from within the experience of the drama creates access to writing in a range of genres and helps children reflect upon and deepen their engagement in the drama. Overheard conversations are employed to create alternative views of the incident, and to show how rumour and gossip spread inaccuracies.

Avoiding the children's suggestions and responses in order to follow the plan may mean that real opportunities for relevant learning are missed. A professional balance between teaching objectives and the children's interests is always required.

Teaching Objectives and Learning Areas
- Work independently in a variety of groups (*personal and social skills*).
- Engage in appropriate questioning, note taking and writing in role (*language*).
- Consider how the drama provides access to different perspectives (*reflection*).

Prior Experience and Materials
No prior experience is necessary, although this would fit well within a literacy focus on reported speech journalism and newspaper articles.
- Copies of the RSPCA report and the newspaper article from the Daily Mail, 1990.
- Large sheets of paper and coloured felts.
- Clipboard and pencils (approx. six).
- Reference books on dogs.

First Encounters: Creating the Drama Context

DOGS

- Begin by discussing dogs with the class, their own and others' dogs, their different kinds, sizes and natures.

- Briefly explain about guard dogs and how, in the early nineties the issue of guard dogs, some of whom were bred to be aggressive, gained media attention. As a result of a number of attacks and the public outcry that followed, new laws were eventually introduced. Give out the newspaper article 'Tough New Code To Put Muzzle on Devil Dogs' and read it together or individually.

- Discuss their reactions to this and their knowledge of the breeds involved, reference books may be helpful here to show pictures and read extracts.

DANGER ON THE PLAYGROUND

- Inform the children that the drama is going to examine an incident reported in the paper at that time, about a loose Rottweiler attacking a child at school, the article was entitled 'Devil Dog Attacks Child'.

- Ask groups to make a freeze frame of the moment of attack, on the playground in lunch break. Make it clear that no one is to be dog, its presence will have to be shown implicitly.

- As a class observe each freeze frame in turn. Move around and touch individuals on the shoulder asking them what they are thinking, saying or doing. Draw the class's attention to any adults such as teachers, dinner ladies, parents, or visitors who are shown.

- In role as a teacher, make an urgent one sided 999 emergency call in front of the class, reporting the attack. Request an ambulance and ask that the police be informed, and come to remove the offending dog, which a member of staff has detained in the caretaker's shed.

- Give out large sheets of paper and felt tips and ask the same groups to make a detailed plan of the school playground where the attack took place. Are there mobile classrooms in the vicinity? Where are the main school buildings and entrances situated? What is beyond the perimeter fences?

- When this has been created in reasonable detail, ask the groups to mark the route that the dog took, showing how it got in, where it came from, and where the child was when the attack took place. Also, ask them to indicate where any members of staff were, were any looking out from the staffroom window and who was supervising in the playground? This scene setting and initial character mapping opportunity, enables groups to create their own narratives around the incident.

THE DOG'S OWNER

- Tell the children that earlier that morning before the incident took place Mrs Dinning, the owner of two pedigree Rottweilers, Dizzy and Daz, had gone as usual on a Monday to purchase dog food from a local shop. Ask them in threes to improvise this scene, in role as the storekeeper, Mrs Dinning and another local customer.

- Allow time for this to be developed, then ask the children to select and prepare a brief extract from it to show to the class. Emphasise you are interested in their ideas, not their acting, and ask them to share a snippet which reveals something about Mrs Dinning.

- Watch several of these, and reflect out loud upon the ideas they generate, eg. Mrs Dinning is tired and unwell due to over work, she has been burgled several times in the last year and needs protection and so on.

Conflicts and Tensions: Developing the Drama

GATHERING EVIDENCE ABOUT THE ATTACK

- Ask the children if this attack happened in their school at morning break, and the child had to be taken to hospital for stitches, what would be the immediate consequences? Would the secretary ring 999? Would the headteacher, the child's parents and the police get involved? Ask pairs to select one of the likely telephone conversations and improvise it in role.

- Suggest that the headteacher is likely to interview the staff on duty to find out what happened. Ask the children in small groups to set up the head's office and prepare to improvise the meeting. Give the children a few minutes to sort out their roles and plan their improvisation. Might the headteacher wonder whether they were doing their playground duty properly. Might the staff be upset? Should the gate have been shut? Suggest some of these thoughts and questions, so that they filter through as options and possibilities whilst the groups are preparing their improvisations.

- As a class, watch extracts from about half the groups and after each one comment reflectively on what you notice, eg. 'The head didn't even offer them a seat, I wonder why?' 'Why did that teacher keep shifting in her seat and mumbling do you think?' Prompt the children to ponder on these improvisations too.

- Suggest that as the head finished talking to the staff, police officers arrived to interview both the adults who'd been present at the incident and the headteacher of the school. Ask the child in each group who took the role of the head in the last improvisation, to become the police officer in this one, the other children remain in the same roles. Gather the officers together and in role as the Superintendent, brief them on the case and hand out clipboards and pencils. This spontaneous improvisation begins as soon as each officer goes to join the group of staff waiting in the head's study.

- Following this, watch brief extracts from the remaining groups and discuss whether this interview differed from that undertaken with the headteacher. Did the adults respond differently to these two figures of authority, one known and one unknown? Ask the children for examples from their drama to illuminate their points, and consider whether different information was offered, and different styles of language used.

- Suggest that the RSPCA visited Mrs Dinning, as they are concerned about the welfare of the animals. Ask the class to take up roles as RSPCA inspectors with you on the hot seat as Mrs Dinning. Answer their questions as you feel appropriate. Probably, like all such owners, she could look after her dogs more carefully or give them more exercise, but whether this incident is her fault is another matter.

PARENTS' VIEWS AT THE GATE

- Inform the children that by mid afternoon the police had also interviewed Mrs Dinning, and had placed both Dizzy and Daz in the police dog pound. At the end of school, the parents at the gate were talking about the attack, although some were hearing about it for the first time. Ask the children to improvise one of these conversations in twos or threes.

- Tell the children that a teacher rushing to a meeting, left the school promptly that day and overheard some of these conversations. Take up the silent role of the supply teacher and move round several groups asking them to gossip when you arrive and stop when you move on. In role, share your thoughts aloud as you leave each group, particularly if the conversations reflect a distortion of the facts as you see them.

WHO IS RESPONSIBLE? WHERE DOES THE BLAME LIE?

- Ask the children to watch you. In role as Mrs Dinning, telephone a friend of yours, another Rottweiler owner, and in a one-sided conversation explain how furious you are the police have impounded Dizzy and Daz. You are also aggrieved that the school does not seem prepared to take some responsibility for the incident. You wonder whether the gates were open, fences broken, children badly behaved, or if the staff were not paying attention? Try to use the ideas the children generated earlier.

- Suggest to the class that the RSPCA, might hold a meeting to air these issues and improve public knowledge about caring for dogs. They might invite Mrs Dinning, the headteacher, local journalists and the staff involved. Let the children decide how to stage this meeting and arrange the furniture accordingly. Do they think anyone else should be present? Offer to be an RSPCA official and chair the proceedings and invite children to volunteer for the various roles. Recommend that the journalists record verbatim quotes or make notes during the press conference, to enable later reports to be written. Give out materials for this. Provide time for the class to suggest possible questions and concerns to voice.

- In role as an RSPCA official, formally open the meeting, express your concern at the situation, comment on the child's condition in hospital, the need to know about breeds of dogs and be conscientious owners and invite questions of information or clarification to members of the panel. Request that everyone state their name and work before they pose questions. Chair the proceedings and at some point fairly early on, offer everyone present, the article 'Devil Dogs?' from your magazine *RSPCA Today*. Make it clear you are not commenting on Mrs Dinning's care of her dogs, but wish everyone to understand the plight of some of these animals. Following this, continue the discussion and, when appropriate, summarise the situation, make recommendations and close the meeting.

Resolutions: Drawing the Drama Together

ALTERNATIVE WRITTEN RECORDS

- Identify with the class the many different places in which the incident might be reported upon in written form. List these on the board. For example:
- different newspapers' reports
- Mrs Dinning's diary entry
- police notes and statement
- the headteacher's report to the governing body
- the RSPCA inspector's report or an RSPCA magazine article
- the parents' formal letter of complaint to the school
- informal letters or emails from the staff on duty to friends

Let each child select one of the written genres suggested and write it, possibly using the computer to produce some of them. Share extracts of these and briefly discuss the various perspectives recorded and the facts and opinions detailed.

CARING FOR POWERFUL DOGS

- Ask small groups to produce a short documentary style television item, either to be shown on *Blue Peter* or *Despatches*, on the issue of caring for large and powerful dogs. This should seek to include the ideas explored in this incident and reflect the need for new and better provision to protect society as well as the dogs.

- Identify together six points which owners of these particular breeds need to bear in mind and which the RSPCA might list in an information pamphlet.
- Discuss as a class how the different drama conventions used, allowed you all to consider the variety of perspectives and standpoints on the issue. You might list a few of these, to help the children learn the names and application of the conventions.

Extension Activities

- Compare the different articles, reports and letters produced. Discuss how facts and opinions were represented, and how purpose and audience influence form and content. Work on reported speech in literacy time would connect to some of this writing.
- Discuss how facts become distorted, how relative the truth is and how all perspectives need to be considered. Do the children have any examples from their lives where an event has been misrepresented or re-viewed by others in the media or in conversation?
- Write to the RSPCA or the PDSA for information about looking after animals and in particular dogs of this kind. Issues of dog registration, quarantine, identification and animal rights could also be explored.

Resourcing Further Drama from Newspapers

Local and national news issues are frequently a rich source for dramatic investigation, although in many cases further information may need to be collected prior to the drama, to enrich the children's understanding and avoid stereotypes being played out. Citizenship issues can also be tackled through news items. Try to avoid letting such dramas rotate around key media figures, but if the class are fascinated by the group Steps or the Spice Girls, for example, then it is possible to examine a similar group's success in an imaginary frame. The media attention, misrepresentations, personal tensions, incessant travelling and so on which surround this group will create an informed parallel examination of a pop group's experience. Different ways to resource drama from newspapers and magazine articles include the following.

1   **Display Newspaper Examples and let the Class select one to Investigate**

    Encourage the children to cut out articles from contemporary magazines or newspapers and display these over several weeks, discussing the issues raised by them. Vote in class to select one for a full dramatic exploration and then plan accordingly.

2   **Focus on a Chosen Issue**

    Identify an issue you want the class to examine (e.g. drugs, bullying, an aspect of citizenship, treatment of the elderly) and collect newspaper articles about this theme. These examples will offer you ideas, real scenarios and a range of arguments about the issue which can help you plan semi-fictional situations and specific predicaments in the drama. Such articles can also be used during the drama, as resources to highlight particular perspectives and provide further information, in a manner similar to the RSPCA report.

3   **Focus on Photographs**

    Offer the children a selection of photographs from newspapers, which might prompt drama. Each group's choice can be created as a freeze frame and then brought briefly to life as an improvisation which can be voted upon as the basis for whole class drama. Again, the actual news article can be read as a contrast to their ideas, and perhaps compared to a news article that they write themselves during the drama.

4   Focus on Headlines

Create a display of powerful headlines without their accompanying articles. The resonance of these provides plenty of scope for interpretation. Each group can choose one and create a freeze frame about it and then the class vote on which title they want to develop in drama. Examples have included a drama about an international espionage ring created from the headline 'Miss Sweet in a Sticky Corner' and a Millwall v Manchester United drama based upon the headline 'Unexploded Bomb!' The genuine news articles are fascinating to read after the drama, and demonstrate the ambiguity intended in many headlines.

Let's play drugs and dealers

TV SHOW NOBODY WATCHED

Young guns

DUMP YOUR BABIES HERE
'Post it' plan for abandoned tots

Deep freeze

Junior football nets millions

Elixir of youth could rejuvenate elderly

Chapter 4

A TRADITIONAL TALE:
OISEEN THE BRAVE - AN IRISH LEGEND

Introduction

This drama uses two fragments of information. The first is the closing paragraph of the accompanying retold tale, Oiseen the Brave, and the second is a quote which seeks to capture one of the themes within the tale, '*He who takes more than his fair share receives his just deserts.*' The drama involves the children in constructing the past life of the dead man, and seeking to align their imaginative flashbacks of his life with this quote as they do so. The teacher as narrator, draws all their ideas and explanations into a coherent tale, which develops as the drama unfolds.

The closing paragraph of the tale, describes the mysterious and unexplained death of a young man, this serves to intrigue the children and prompt the dramatic investigation. The class seek to establish where this event took place and to build a sense of the community in which the young man dies. In role as villagers, the class respond to his demise, gossip about it, search his saddle-bags for clues, and begin to develop perceptions about his life which is examined. In this drama there is no search for closure or one agreed narrative thread, although you could choose to agree one version and develop it further. In the session(s) described the meanings are left open and the story of his life remains ambiguous. The retold tale included is developed from a version in Betty Rosen's book *Shapers and Polishers* (1991 Mary Glasgow). The tale may be read at the close of the drama or on another occasion, after the children have written their own versions.

The drama convention of **flashback** is highlighted here, alongside **overhead conversations** and **teacher as storyteller**. Flashbacks (either in the form of freeze frames or as improvisations) are used to look into the young man's past and construct significant events which may have influenced his life. Overhead conversations expose the rumours and gossip, which surround unusual events and indicate how anecdotes grow out of proportion, fed by opinion and exaggeration. With the teacher in storyteller mode, the children's ideas can be honoured and retold as the story unfolds. The use of this convention can also add atmosphere and tension to the drama.

Avoiding the children's suggestions and responses in order to follow the plan may mean that real opportunities for relevant learning are missed. A professional balance between teaching objectives and children's interests is always required.

Teaching Objectives and Learning Areas
- Develop spontaneous ideas in a creative manner (*the imagination*).
- Use language to retell events, speculate, and reason in role (*language*).
- Consider their drama, its content and process (*reflection*).

Prior Experience and Materials
This drama would fit well within a focus upon traditional tales, myths and legends. It would be preferable not to tell the tale prior to the drama, so the class are free to construct their own versions.
- An easel or flip chart with the quote upon it.
- Six large sheets of paper and felt pens.
- Paper and pencils for each group.

First Encounters: Creating the Drama Context

SETTING THE SCENE

- Tell the class you are going to offer them two significant pieces of information, one oral and the other written, from which their drama will evolve.

- Tell the concluding section of the story in a slightly fuller form - without naming Oiseen, but describe the extraordinary event, and voice the villager's perspectives. *'It was market day and the small town was a real hub of activity - everyone was selling and buying, bartering and gossiping, so at first no one noticed the stranger riding down the hill towards them. But as his horse's hooves began to clatter on the cobblestones, folk nudged one another, and silence began to fall. Who was this handsome young man, with the purple plumed helmet, astride a fine white stallion? Where had he come from? Whom had he come to meet? The people watched with interest for as he looked closely at each one of them, he seemed to be searching for someone, they knew not who. Then his eyes alighted on the old stone water trough, and smiling with pleasure, he reined his horse in, swung his feet out of the stirrups and stepped down onto the ground. All at once, his body began to shiver and shake, quiver and quake and his smooth skin creased into layers of wrinkles and seemed to fade. His veins surfaced, blue and bulging, and his stature diminished as he shrank visibly and horribly. Then he slumped to the ground and lay dead and lifeless before them on the cobbles.'*

- Pause, then read the quote, previously placed on the easel, *'He who takes more than his fair share receives his just desserts.'*

- Ask the children to connect these two pieces of information and discuss what it all means in pairs.

- Suggest to the class that you make a map of the place where the fatal incident happened. Discuss the options with them, what country did it happen in, was it in the past or the present, in a town or village and so on. Agree some of these elements and then create with the children, a large map on the easel. Let the class suggest the physical features and landmarks, as well as the stalls/houses/inns/school and so on. Draw these yourself, perhaps naming some or using symbols to show e.g. the blacksmiths, the church or a fruit stall. Ensure one of the dwellings near the cobbled square, is owned by a wealthy family who could also be the Lord of the Manor. Once a clear sense of the place has been established, move on.

THAT FATEFUL MARKET DAY

- Generate a quick oral list together of folk who live in the community, and who might have been in and around the square on the day that the young man arrived. Suggestions will be dependent on the era, but have included, drunks and vagabonds, town criers and travellers, priests and paupers, local traders, criminals in the stocks, youngsters playing and so on.

- Suggest that just before the incident happened, the Lady of the Manor was looking out of her window at the scene and saw the market stalls buzzing, folk bartering and selling, and children chasing one another. Ask the class to take up a role as one of the villagers, and improvise the scene she saw, using the map to position themselves appropriately.

- Go into role yourself as a travelling pedlar, selling lucky heather or pots and pans, and move among them offering your wares and striking up brief conversations with the villagers.

- Allow this busy scene to evolve for a few minutes, and then freeze everyone and move around quickly asking several individuals what they're doing. Make further enquiries of a few of the villagers e.g. how much are your eggs, or why are you in the stocks, what are you drinking?

- Tell the class that when their class improvisation resumes in a minute, you are going to interrupt it to narrate the arrival of the young man on the horse. Ask them to suggest to each other what they might do or say when the young man dies. Allow a few moments to discuss this, then count down from 5 to 1 and let the class return to the market scene.

Conflicts and Tensions: Developing the Drama

A DEATH AMONG US.

- Interrupt by retelling the same snippet from the end of the tale. As you do, use your eyes to look slowly and searchingly in their faces, as if you are the young man arriving in the town, but use your hands to gesture his demise on the ground before you.

- In role, as the travelling pedlar, express your shock and concern; this is a bad omen for the village. Draw the villagers into this whole class improvisation. What should be done? Dare we touch him? Has he the plague? Does anyone know him? Through posing questions and wondering aloud about the consequences of this death, you will provoke debate and discussion. Let this response take its course and if the class find it too challenging, you could repeat the incident, building on their initial ideas.

- As storyteller of their ideas and actions, relate the different thoughts expressed by the villagers and the actions taken, and end by commenting that the whole community could talk of nothing else. Retell, e.g. *That in the street and the ale house everyone tried to explain his death, for when the young man died that day some of the villagers felt he was diseased, unclean and refused to touch him, while others believed he had come in search of someone. A few of their number claimed his death was a bad omen for the village. Whatever their reasons, no-one was prepared to move him, so that night whilst the body still lay in the square, only covered by a blanket thrown over it, the villagers talked about this mysterious death.*

- Ask the children in groups of three or four, to gossip as villagers about the man, where had he come from, what was he looking for, did anyone know him, why had he come to this town?

- Suggest that if a stranger had been in the village that night, he would have overheard a lot of these conversations. Listen to a few brief snatches of these, and emphasise that you're listening for their ideas and explanations.

WHO WAS THIS MAN?

- As storyteller continue to build their ideas into the tale, and inform them that even as the villagers were gossiping that night, a few of their number had crept out to search for clues in the young man's saddlebag.

- Hand out large sheets of paper and pens and ask groups to draw what was found inside. Ponder aloud a few possibilities eg. a vial, a map, etchings, a locket, and a note or a sealed letter. Once they've settled down to the task, tour the groups providing paper to write the actual letter, or part of a note found in his saddlebag. Remind them that the quote on the easel might help them, as they seek to construct reasons why the young man came to the village.

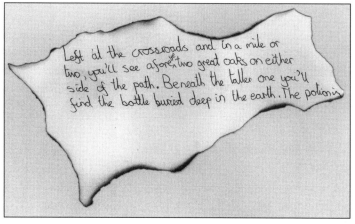

Shannon (aged 9)

- Let each group show the class their drawings of the saddlebag's contents and conjecture about the possible history of the objects in it and how they came to be in the saddlebag. The written notes or letter should also be read aloud. Highlight any connections between the objects and ideas shared by the different groups eg. it may be that several groups believe that a woman is involved, or that the man had committed a crime or was following instructions.
- As a class, discuss how the various drama conventions used so far have enabled you to build up a sense of the young man's identity.
- Ask the class in twos or threes to create the young man's last conversation. Where was he last night or early in the morning, and to whom did he talk? Listen to extracts of some of these.
- Suggest that as his body shrank and he knew he was going to die, memories of his life flashed before his eyes and significant events in his past surfaced like a film. Ask the class to create group flashbacks, either as an improvisation or a freeze frame, of a moment in the man's life when he had to make an important decision.
- As a class, observe each of these freeze frames or brief improvisations and discuss together any common themes.
- These could be written up as paragraphs, literary flashbacks in the narrative, by pairs in the small groups. Remind them to weave in the quote as a subtext.
- If you want to extend the drama you could now agree one event in his past and flesh this out in more detail, exploring the incident through the use of different conventions. Then seeking through further drama to construct his life history.

Resolutions: Drawing the Drama Together

A FITTING EPITAPH

- Ask the children to create a fitting epitaph for the man, as a group sculpture or a freeze frame, reflecting the main theme in his life and death.

Love sustained me.

- Once they are working on this go round and ask each group to add a title to their sculpture. Observe these altogether and hear the titles offered.

Greed and Violence.

- Gather the class together and comment upon the diversity and commonality of the ideas shared. Observe that the drama session may be closing, but the meanings are left open. All their ideas are possible. His life remains uncertain, shrouded in mystery.

A life for a life.

- Discuss which of the drama conventions revealed most about the main character, and comment on the relationship between the form and content developed through the conventions.

He always wanted more.

- Either immediately, or within a week or so, tell/read the class the story of Oiseen the Brave. Afterwards encourage small group discussion of the tale and the different life histories which emerged in their drama. Re-focus upon the quote '*He who takes more than his fair share receives his just desserts*' and discuss the evidence of this within the Irish legend and in their narratives.

One bad deed creates another.

(9/10 year olds)

Extension Activities

- Construct group retellings with each child contributing a written paragraph to the group's collectively composed tale, using the ideas developed in the drama.
- Explore the legend of Oiseen the Brave in literacy work, highlighting the legendary character, the element of fantasy, the repetitive language, the use of warnings and the number three, as well as other linguistic features of this genre.

- Read more of the fascinating Irish folktales about Oiseen and his family, for instance his upbringing in the mountains, how his father Finn found him and about his mother the fair lady of Allen, in Eileen O' Faoilan's *Irish Folk Myths and Legends*, Penguin.

- Examine themes in other traditional tales, and get the class to find or design proverbs or quotes to highlight the issues they examine.

- Read *The Man Who Wanted To Live Forever* retold by Selina Hastings (1991, Walker) and compare and contrast the narratives.

Resourcing Further Drama from Traditional Tales

Traditional tales, folk and fairy stories, myths and legends offer rich resource material for classroom drama. They often have clear characters, explore key areas of human understanding, as well as the journey into adulthood and are packed with narrative action. It is preferable to choose tales for dramatic exploration which are unknown to the class, since this avoids re-enactment and the sometimes dampening effect which well known tales can have upon older children. With the wealth of tales available in both picture book form and in short story collections, quality tales can easily be found and several printed versions of the same story can be examined to contrast with the children's co-authored creation. It helps if the teacher operates as storyteller and can weave the children's ideas and insights into the unfolding tale, as this provides both coherence and atmosphere. Visual images from illustrated texts can also be used to enrich the children's thinking. There are different ways of using traditional tales, including the following options.

1   Using the Tale to Guide the Drama

This involves the teacher telling the tale, but stopping intermittently during the telling to ask the children how they could find out more about the characters, issues or conflicts in the story. After some dramatic exploration and investigation, the story is taken up again and the children's ideas are woven into the retelling. In this way the story guides and provokes the drama, which expands upon the narrative and enriches the children's understanding of the tale. This is a useful strategy for less experienced drama teachers as the story provides the structural security of a plan, but offers plenty of space for innovation, extension and imagination. We recommend the following tales.

SELKIE GIRL

RETOLD BY SUSAN COOPER

The Selkie Girl, retold by Susan Cooper (1991) MacMillan
This haunting tale, tells of a young man who tricks a Selkie girl into marrying him, he hides her seal skin and thus prevents her returning to the sea. She bears him children but eventually a fateful ending of their marriage comes to pass. The visuals are useful prompts to help heighten particular elements in the drama, which explore love and loss, culture and identity. Another version is found in *The Broonies, Silkies and Fairies* by Duncan Williamson (1989), Cannongate.

Never Let Go, Geraldine McCaughrean (1998) Hodder
This Scottish fairytale, fabulously illustrated by Jason Cockcroft, describes plain Janet's attempt to rescue her young love Tamlin from the Fairy Queen's clutches. She is put to the test many times but resolves never to let him go. The tale offers the class the chance to explore fear and determination in a fantasy world where the blood of all the world's wars runs ankle deep. Another version entitled *Tamlane*, is found in *Tales of Wonder and Magic* collected by B. Doherty (1997), Walker, and another in *Clever Gretchen and other Forgotten Folktales*, by A. Lurie, (1980), Mammoth.

The Orphan Boy, Tololwa M. Mollel (1990) Clarion Books
This Maasai legend explains why the planet Venus is known to the Maasai as Kileken, the orphan boy. A lonely old man takes in an orphan, who seems mysteriously to solve some of the problems of the drought. The man cannot rest until the boy's secret powers are explained, despite his agreement to accept the situation and not to pry. This tale examines strength and weakness, youth and age as well as the consequences of broken trust.

Ladder to the Sky, retold by Barbara J Esbensen (1989) Little, Brown and Company
This is a legend of the Ojibway or Chippewan people of North America, which explores the fall of man and seeks to explain how and why medicines were first invented. One member of a village seems favoured by the spirits, so the jealous villagers take the matter into their own hands. This tale lends itself to guiding a drama as it is packed with rumours and conflicts, and has considerable open-ended potential.

2   Building from a Story Fragment

The teacher selects an extract from the story to share and the class build upon this part of the story, investigating prior events, consequences and the motives, behaviours, and emotions of the characters. Together they dig down into the layers of the tale they are constructing which will be connected in some elemental fashion to the 'original' tale. After the drama, the tale chosen by the teacher can be shared as another version and similarities and differences explored, so in effect the drama prefigures the tale in some way. The opening or closing sections can be used or a couple of episodes within the tale, this is how *Oiseen the Brave* was used. The story fragment provides a dramatic context, but the drama itself shapes the narrative which the class co-author together. The issues which a traditional tale examines can also be used to resource a drama, so the dramatic investigation prefigures the text, mirroring its central concern in another context. This enables the class to bring increased empathy and understanding to these issues when the text is read or studied after the drama. Writing in role or writing scenes of the action as a play script can easily be prompted through such drama. We recommend the following tales.

The Green Children, Kevin Crossley Holland (1994) Oxford University Press.
A powerful English folk tale based upon events in the 12th century, when Suffolk villagers found a green boy and girl on the edge of Woolpit, Suffolk. This mysterious happening, the identity of the children, and the consequences for the village can be examined through drama. Issues of difference, fear, prejudice and loneliness are explored here. This tale works well as an opening fragment, which provides a mystery, tension and a predicament that needs to be solved, or a drama prefiguring the issues within it can be developed.

The Glass Garden, Joyce Dunbar (1999) Frances Lincoln.
This tale tells of how Lorenzo, the finest glassmaker in Venice seeks to protect his only daughter by building a glass garden for her to dwell in. Trapped in this beautiful, but limited world, Lucia thinks about the world outside. A regular theme in folklore, this works well in drama, providing endless possibilities for action and reflection, in its examination of parental roles and responsibilities. A parallel tale entitled, The Paper Garden, can be found in *Breaking the Spell: Tales of Enchantment*, (1997) selected by S. Grindley, Kingfisher.

The Changeling, Malachy Doyle (1999) Pont Books.
This Welsh folktale, tells of a farming couple who have one of their twins taken from them by the Tylwyth Teg, the fairy folk and a changeling put in his place. By setting the scene with the ambiguous beginning of this tale, the class can explore the consequences for the family, the magical world that young Ifan is brought up in and the issues of love and loss. Who will the young couple consult, what might they do and how will they feel towards the changeling?

'Two Brothers', Inno Sorsy (1995) in *The River That Went To The Sky: Twelve Tales by African Storytellers*, Mr Medlicott, Kingfisher.
This West African story explores two sons' responses to their father's death; the elder brother asserts his age and authority over the younger brother who misses his father and struggles to find his feet in the world. Try telling the opening and relate the discord between them and let the drama develop from there. Will the class seek a resolution in unity or eventual separation?

3   Revisiting the Tale after the Telling

The tale is first told in its entirety and then parts of it are revisited and elaborated upon through drama. There are inevitably gaps in tales, moments of indecision which are left undeveloped, characters whose conversation remains unrecorded, and stretches of narrative time which hardly receive a mention. These unwritten and unspoken elements can be fleshed out through drama and serve to deepen the children's understanding of the issues beneath the tale. Following the reading or telling of a tale, the class can be asked to identify parts of the story which interested or puzzled them. Their questions are listed on the board, and become the focus for the drama, so the class unravel intriguing and undeveloped elements in the tale. Sometimes particular characters are highlighted and their life histories explored or new tales of their later adventures created through drama. Modern parallels and analogies can also be created, building upon the themes and character traits shown in the first tale. We recommend the following tales.

The Weaving of a Dream, retold by Marilee Heyer (1989) Puffin.
This Chinese folktale of the Chuang Brocade tells how a poor young widow weaves a beautiful tapestry, but on completion has it taken from her by the fairies. Her three sons seek in turn to bring it back for her, but only the youngest is able to undertake this task, the others are tempted by money and the bright lights of the city. Revisiting this tale involves examining hopes and dreams and perhaps fleshing out an autobiography for the wise old crone who plays a pivotal role in the story and offers the sons their heart's desires.

Sir Gawain and the Loathy Lady, retold by S. Hastings (1987) Walker.
This tale, explores the chivalry and loyalty expected of the legendary knights of King Arthur's Round Table. The tale could also be used to guide a drama, but it works well as a tale to examine parallel themes in modern times about what women really desire and deserve in life. The dramatic investigation will enrich the children's understanding of the tale, and is likely to focus on gender issues and women's roles, examining stereotypes and the children's experiences.

'Prince Ivan, the Witch Baby and the Little Sister of the Sun' in *Old Peter's Russian Tales*, Arthur Ransome (1916) Jonathon Cape.
An adventurous Russian narrative, which involves Prince Ivan in searching for the end of the world, where he can live in safety from his sister, who is a witch baby with iron teeth. He befriends several giants on his journeys to and from the Castle of the Little Sister of the Sun, and finally with their help outwits his sister. Children have identified questions about destiny and parent's roles and responsibilities from this story.

'An Old Man Who Saved Some Ungrateful People' in *Children of Wax: African Folk Tales*, Alexander McCall Smith (1989), Canongate.

This folktale from Matabeleland, explores issues of distrust as a group of villagers fear one man's wisdom and knowledge, yet need his help. In many ways a simple story, it highlights peer pressure and is a relatively easy tale to update, investigating the children's questions in a more contemporary setting.

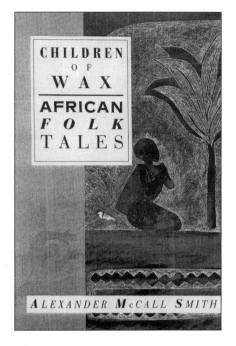

A Traditional Tale
Oiseen the Brave

I want to tell you a story about the Land of the Ever Young and about the only man who ever lived in that land of milk and honey and here in the land of mortal men. Oiseen the Brave was a bright young man, with eyes as blue as Galway Bay itself when no clouds float over it, and a smile as deep and sure as the ocean bed. Oiseen was fit and strong, with many a friend and very few foes. He lived life to the full, drinking until he could sup no more, eating until his belly groaned, and singing and dancing until his voice was raw and his feet were sore. He had been born into money and did not need to labour on the land, instead he enjoyed the many pleasures of living and particularly the excitement of the hunt, indeed oftentimes he would pursue deer in and out of the forests, returning triumphantly with his prize. He was carefree ... blessed one might say, with a sunny disposition and the means to maintain it.

Now, one day as I recall, Oiseen and his friends were out hunting together when they happened upon a great white stag–a magnificent creature it was too, which led them a merry dance through the forest. Hither and thither it ran, in and out of the undergrowth and up and down hill and dale. Their surefooted horses followed at a swift pace but were unable to catch up with the stag, until that is, it allowed itself to be cornered in a clearing on the very edge of the cliff. As the young men drew back their arrows, the stag outwitted them, by leaping from the cliff and plunging into the waters below. It swam out, it swam deep until just the tips of its antlers pricked the surface of the water. They watched amazed, as the stag clambered onto a rocky pinnacle in the ocean and then turned slowly to face them. Its dark eyes seemed to stare unblinkingly at the young men, who stood immobile, captured in its gaze.

The following day, Oiseen's friends gathered together again to hunt for this extraordinary white stag. They found it easily, perhaps too easily, was it waiting for them they wondered...? Hither and thither it ran, in and out of the undergrowth and up and down hill and dale, until it emerged for the second time into the clearing on the very edge of the cliff. Again it leapt from the cliff and plunged into the waters below. It swam out, it swam deep until just the tips of its antlers pricked the surface of the water. Then it clambered onto the rocky pinnacle and turned to stare deep into the eyes of Oiseen the Brave. Intrigued, Oiseen stared back, captivated by its glare. That night, as he tossed and turned in a fitful sleep, he felt he was again looking into the eyes of the stag and beholding some mysterious and unknown world.

On the third day, the young men plotted to capture the creature, Oiseen drew the shortest straw and so it was he who swam out to the rocky pinnacle and awaited the arrival of the stag. His friends chased it through the forest, hither and thither it ran, in and out of the undergrowth up and down hill and dale, until it reached the clearing on the cliff edge. It pawed its feet and snorted disdainfully at the young men, then leapt from the cliff and plunged into the water below. It swam out, it swam deep, until just the tips of its antlers pricked the surface of the water. When it clambered onto the rocks, Oiseen stepped boldly forward and grasped the stag's antlers, but in a single movement the great creature tossed him onto its broad wet flanks and plunged down into the dark waters. Oiseen was seen no more.

The stag took Oiseen down to the Land of the Ever Young, the land of Tir-Nan-Oge, the enchanted land of no time at all. Now if you or I wished to travel there, it would take us one hundred years and a day. Too long, too late, too old we would be to dwell in the Land of the Ever Young. And yet there are some who say it is not there, but in the here and now, perhaps it is ... perhaps for some maybe. As Oiseen dwelt behind the antlers of the stag, it seemed as if no time passed, for twenty years might pass in our world but there would have little more than an hour passed. Oiseen remained both young and strong and enjoyed pleasure aplenty, learning much about beauty and truth in this mysterious paradise, yet still it seemed Oiseen searched for more.

One morning, he heard a woman singing and the tune reminded him of the lullabies his mother had sung to him years before, he realised he missed her and desired to see her again. He went at once to the 'Powers that Be' in Tir-Nan-Oge and demanded that he should be allowed to return to see his family once more. They tried to explain to him that his parents had passed on long since, but Oiseen knew this was not true, for he was still young and surely little time had passed. Finally, Oiseen was granted his wish and offered a fine white stallion and a helmet with a single purple plume. However the 'Powers that Be' in Tir-Nan-Oge warned him never to touch the mortal soil on his journey or he would be unable to return to the Land of the Ever Young.

So Oiseen set out, and travelled many a mile in full expectation of meeting his parents and friends again. Through forests and deserts he journeyed, up and down hill and dale, until finally he saw a trickle stream, which he recognised from his childhood, leading down into a village.

It was market day in the village and many were the folk who'd turned out to barter and to banter. Eagerly young Oiseen searched the face of each one in turn, but recognised not one amongst their number. Disappointed, he turned his horse to leave, when his eyes alighted on an old stone water trough there on the cobbles. Here, he knew he had slaked his thirst as a lad, splashed his friends in the heat of the day and led many a horse to drink after a day's hunting. The crystal clear water twinkled in the sunlight and seemed to beckon him forwards, so he climbed eagerly out of the saddle. But the instant his boots touched the cobbles, it seemed as if the years that he'd lived in Tir-Nan-Oge passed over him in but a moment. His veins surfaced, blue and broken, his skin began to wrinkle and fade and his stature diminished alarmingly. His body shivered and shook and then he slumped to the ground, dead and lifeless there on the cobbles.

Chapter 5

A NOVEL: *THE ANGEL FROM NITSHILL ROAD*
BY ANNE FINE

Introduction

This drama is based upon the concerns and themes examined in Anne Fine's novel *The Angel from Nitshill Road* (1992, Mammoth). The story is used to provide a context in which the class co-author new chapters of the text through drama. In effect, having heard the first two chapters, the children establish possible narrative actions in harmony with the plot and the characters, and dig down into the internal dynamics of the situation to examine the central issue of the text. Flashbacks and flashforwards in time are used to avoid building a linear narrative composed only of action. A poem by Adrian Mitchell, on the same theme, *Back in the Playground Blues* is also read during this drama to intensify the emotional engagement through its condensed, yet explicit imagery.

The novel examines the issue of bullying and the relationships between the children who live in fear of the class bully; Barry Hunter and his gang. A new girl, Celeste, arrives at Nitshill Road School and over time the situation alters, so that by the time she leaves, even their teacher, the weak Mr Fairway, has begun to assert his authority and to live up to his name at last. The drama involves the class in examining the predicament and feelings of the bullied children, of their teacher and of Barry Hunter himself.

The drama convention **decision alley** is highlighted in this chapter. This is a convention for examining a character's inner thoughts and conflicting concerns at a moment of tension or decision making. It involves the class forming two lines facing inwards, between which a character from the drama walks. The child walks down this 'alley' and listens to their own conscience or thoughts and then decides what action to take. This develops empathy and insight and stresses the complexity, conflicts and compromise often involved in decision making. Other conventions, including **thought tracking** and **choral chanting** are also highlighted. In the former, the class creates and reflects upon the inner voices and thoughts of a variety of different characters, whose fears and feelings are heard. In the latter, the children invent word patterns, phrases or chants which, when repeatedly intoned, evoke atmosphere and add mood. In this drama the choral chants are part of one character's recurring nightmare.

Avoiding the children's suggestions and responses in order to follow the plan may mean that real opportunities for relevant learning are missed. A professional balance between teaching objectives and children's interests is always required.

Teaching Objectives and Learning Areas

- Engage with their own and others' feelings and shape the drama accordingly (*personal and social skills*).

- Use conventions with increasing understanding of the form (*the drama process*).

- Discuss the issue of bullying in the fictional context of the drama (*the content of the drama*).

Prior Experience and Materials

The first two chapters of *The Angel from Nitshill Road* need to have been read to the class prior to the drama.

- Easel, paper and pen
- Writing materials for each child

First Encounters: Creating the Drama Context

LIVING IN FEAR

- Through discussion, remind the children of *'the three terribly unhappy children at Nitshill Road School; Penny, Mark and Marigold'* who are described in the first two chapters. Reflect upon the arrival of Celeste and discuss the incident when she bites Barry Hunter in chapter two.

- Explain to the class that through your drama you are going to explore the character Marigold, and her fears and concerns. Re-read the description of her on pages 10 – 13, and ponder together briefly on her attitude to school.

- Ask the children in threes to role play Marigold and her Mum and Dad at breakfast on a school morning – does she try to avoid going to school? Share a few snippets of their improvisations, and make brief comments upon them yourself, encouraging the children also to comment.

- Tell the children that Marigold's fears of Barry Hunter and his gang surface in her dreams. Ask them to create one of these nightmares as a group improvisation, in which she doesn't actually see Barry or his gang, but feels their presence in a dream that represents her fears. Suggest they might like to include a repetitive ritual chant or sound to this representation.

- Observe, listen and interpret each one of these with the class. What do the choral chants and actions reveal about Marigold and her past experiences?

"THE KILLING GROUND"

- Ask the children in the same small groups to create a freeze frame of the playground at Nitshill Road School one typical lunchtime, when Marigold is suffering the usual verbal taunts, and her worst nightmares seem to be coming true.

- Count down from 5 to 1 to help the groups quieten, then each group creates their freeze frame simultaneously. When they're ready tell them you are going to go around and touch individuals, to ask what they're thinking or saying as the character they are portraying. Ask them to speak out loud when you come to them to make clear whether they are the bullied, a member of the bully's gang or an onlooker. Listen to at least one person in each group.

- Suggest to the class they can change roles, if they wish, to make a whole class freeze-frame of the playground at a moment when bullying is going on, and then ask them to adopt positions accordingly. When they are in position, read Adrian Mitchell's poem: *Back in the Playground Blues*.

- Conclude your reading by going on to narrate that the class teacher, Mr Fairway and a colleague, Mrs Cooper were at that very moment looking out from the staffroom window. Ask the children to role-play in pairs the conversation that the two of them have, drawing upon what they know of the children involved, and what they think they can or should do. Either pair the children yourself or let them choose, and allow time to consider the conversation before they improvise it. Then listen to a few snippets of these.

- Through shared or paired writing, record an entry together in Marigold's private diary that evening, which expresses what she feels about her day. Does she think she can tell a teacher her fears and experiences or would that be telling tales?

Conflicts and Tensions: Developing the Drama

MR FAIRWAY'S DILEMMA

- As narrator, relate that on the way to school the next day, Mr Fairway observes Marigold walking to school nervously and tearfully and wonders what to do. He drives round the block a couple of times and then parks in school. He cannot decide how to handle the situation. Does he have evidence or is it mere conjecture that Marigold is being bullied? Discuss with the children the options open to Mr Fairway. What do they think a concerned teacher would/should do about the situation?

- Ask the class to create a decision alley to investigate Mr Fairway's dilemma. Two lines facing each other can represent the path to the school door, and one child in role as Mr Fairway must walk down the path and listen to his thoughts spoken out loud by the two lines of children. Set this up quite formally, and give the children time to talk to their neighbour in the line, to generate ideas for what they are going to say. Remind the child playing Mr Fairway, that they'll need to walk slowly and listen carefully in order to make up their mind on the basis of what they hear. Tell them you'll want to know their decision.

- When the child as Mr Fairway reaches the 'door' of the school, place them on the hot seat, and allow the class to ask questions. What has this teacher done in the past in these kinds of situations, what's he going to do now and why?

- Through role-play in pairs, improvise one part of Mr Fairway's decision, for example he may decide to have an individual interview with Barry Hunter, with Marigold, or the new girl, Celeste, or even their parents. Alternatively he may discuss his concerns with the headteacher, Mrs Brown, or a colleague. Listen to snippets of these.

THE BULLY HIMSELF

- In role as Barry Hunter, the bully, put yourself in the hot seat with the children as your questioners. Give them some time to prepare questions to put to you. In this questioning, you will need to create a complex picture of the bully, that includes not only the possible causes of his behaviour, but also his vulnerable points and weaknesses. Perhaps he has been bullied himself or is in a home where his parents are very harsh with him. The children need to recognise that he is not omnipotent and that there are ways to combat such bullies. Almost more importantly, explain to them that the children from Nitshill's responses have partly helped you, Barry, to become the powerful gang leader you are and now you want to retain this position. You are used to it and kind of comfortable with this role.

- Having heard you in the hot-seat, ask the children in groups to sum up Barry Hunter's character and what 'makes him tick', how do they think he should be dealt with by the school, and how should they behave with him, and other potential bullies to minimise future similar situations.

- Suggest that as a consequence of all these discussions, Mr Fairway meet with his class, 4C without the key characters, Barry, Celeste or Marigold. Tell the children you're going to leave the room and when you return you'll be in role as Mr Fairway and they will be members of class 4C, but no one is to be one of these three key characters. In role as Mr Fairway, explain that this conversation is necessary to help you be fair to everyone and ask the class to be honest and tell you the truth. Assure them they can trust you and ask them what they know about what's been going on between Barry, Marigold and Celeste. If the children are not very forthcoming help them by offering extra knowledge and support eg. '*Samantha, don't you live next door to Marigold? Does she seem very quiet at home?*' Or '*Has anything like this ever happened before at Nitshill, as you know I'm new round here…*' and so on. In role, discuss with the issues with them as if you were the class teacher in this situation, frame the options, and share how you see matters, inviting their response. Close the meeting as Mr Fairway.

Resolutions: Drawing the Drama Together

LEARNING TO STAND TALL

- Discuss with the children how the members of the fictional class might help Marigold and other classmates like Penny and Mark, become more confident and assertive.
- Suggest that several weeks later, class 4C is on an outing when Marigold, coming out of the museum shop, notices Barry Hunter standing menacingly between her and her friends. Again create a decision alley: what is Marigold thinking; will she ask him to move, will she confront him, call out or go another way? Allow preparation time, and then with a child in role

as Marigold, let her walk down the path created by the two lines of children, listening to the arguments in her head, expressed by the children. Ask Marigold her decision and ascertain why she's chosen this course of action.

- As individuals, ask the children to make an entry in Marigold's diary that night.

- Ask for volunteers to read extracts of these aloud – discuss some of the issues raised and the perspectives described. Is Marigold learning to stand tall, has she more confidence to talk to others about her predicament?

> Today at the science museum BH was after me again, he triped me up when we were in the shop and then he was walking outside. I looked at him and he sneered at me, so i went back in to find some of the others. They'd all gone except mr Fairway and mrs Brown so i went and hung around them. When we came out Mrs Brown said was everything alright? i said yes, but i think she knew 'cos she squeezed my hand. She wants to see me tomorrow. What am i going to say?

Jack (aged 9)

- Comment upon their drama and their ideas about partial resolutions or possible developments. Connect this back to Anne Fine's novel, will she have taken the same routes and prompted Marigold to behave in the same way? Discuss the options open to Anne Fine as an author. Were these parallel in their drama work?

> The Science Trip today was good especially the part on the body. Mr Fairway said he liked my diagrams. On the way out I bought a notebook and some fudge. Barry was standing on the path, waiting for me. At first I wanted to run back in and find some of the others, but he was on his own none of his gang was about. He hadn't bought anything he never had any money. I don't know what made me, but I started walking up to him and said 'Do you want some?' I thought he'd spit it, but he hesitated for a moment then grabbed a piece and kind of smiled. I didn't wait to hear if he liked it I just walked on. He didn't call after me, HE DIDN'T CALL AFTER ME! HE DIDN'T CALL AFTER ME!

Chloe (aged 10)

Extension Activities

- Provide the children with a list of the chapter titles, and on this basis predict how Anne Fine handles the bullying issue. Compare this to their own ideas and possible resolutions.

- Later in the novel, write another diary entry for Marigold. This could highlight interesting comparisons with their earlier entries.

- In Chapter 7, Celeste creates 'A Book of Deeds' in which she records the actions and words of Barry Hunter, to provide evidence against him. New entries could be written and the children's increasingly confident response to these incidents could be created through small group improvisations.

- Discuss Adrian Mitchell's poem *Back in the Playground Blues* in guided reading or a literature circle.

- Establish a circle time focus on peer pressure and being bullied.

BACK IN THE PLAYGROUND BLUES

Dreamed I was in a school playground, I was about four feet high
Yes dreamed I was back in the playground, and standing about
four feet high
The playground was three miles long and the playground was
five miles wide.

It was broken black tarmac with a high fence all around
Broken black dusty tarmac with a high fence running all around
And it had a special name to it; they called it The Killing Ground

Got a mother and a father, they're a thousand miles away
The Rulers of The Killing Ground are coming out to play
Everyone thinking: who they going to play with today?

> You get it for being Jewish
> Get it for being black
> Get it for being chicken
> Get it for fighting back
> You get it for being big and fat
> Get it for being small
> O those who get it get it and get it
> For any damn thing at all

Sometimes they take a beetle, tear off its six legs one by one
Beetle on its black back rocking in the lunchtime sun
But a beetle can't beg for mercy, a beetle's not half the fun.

Heard a deep voice talking, it had that iceberg sound;
"It prepares them for Life" - but I have never found
Any place in my life that's worse than The Killing Ground.

Adrian Mitchell

Resourcing Further Drama from Novels

Novels provide excellent resource material for initiating and framing drama. The narrative provides the people, place and plenty of predicaments. It frames the dramatic action and seeks to explore the characters, their behaviour and motivation in the present, as well as their past lives, and the issues arising in the tale. Re-enactment of a known narrative is not sought, but scenes, or gaps in the narrative, which have not been written by the author, can be improvised so particular individual's perspectives can be examined and elaborated, leading to additional text being co-authored through drama. In this way, the ambiguity and uncertainty, which accompanies real living can be addressed, experienced, and handled appropriately.

Such work feeds easily into writing, both in the same genre, and in an another style that represents the narrative from an alternative viewpoint or stance. Classroom drama focused upon 'what happens next?' in the novel being read or studied, should be used sparingly, but creating earlier scenarios and exploration promotes speculation and reflection, and raises questions about the characters. Such drama helps the children explore both the text and the subtext. Novels can be employed in classroom drama in a variety of ways.

1   **Co-authoring a new Chapter or Event in the Novel**

During the reading/study of a novel, the class can build upon their knowledge and understanding of the characters and events unravelled so far, by creating another chapter (perhaps with the author's title) in the narrative. This could build on the literary convention of flashbacks and examine earlier episodes in individual's lives or explore themes within the real time of the novel. This is how *The Angel from Nitshill Road* is used in this drama. In effect the critical issues in the novel are examined through developing previous or future action, and knowledge about the characters in imaginary contexts.

2   **Relying on a Chapter to Guide the Drama**

Select a chapter to explore for omissions, implications and inferences, as well as extensions. Read up to this chapter and then let the chosen chapter guide you to use drama conventions to examine the character's motives, attitudes and concerns. Read and stop intermittently, inviting the children to suggest how more can be found out about particular individuals or what questions they'd like to ask. Take up their ideas in drama and enrich the language of the unsaid in the text by creating conversations, improvisations and involvement. In this way, the subtext and the text itself is made more explicit as the chapter guides the drama and the children shape their own understanding of the story through their questions and interests. The emphasis is upon character and motivation rather than upon events and actions.

3   **Co-authoring a Follow up Tale**

Having read the complete novel, the class can explore the long-term consequences of the narrative for one or more of the characters. Flashforwards in time, reflections upon the past expressed in the future, and unresolved or incomplete endings can all be examined. Exploring ways in which the past shapes the future and constructing analogies of the text is demanding but intriguing work.

The following novels are recommended for dramatic investigation and have been used in a variety of ways. It is clear, however, that many novels offer opportunities to open up the narrative through drama and dig down into the layers of the text.

Rachel Anderson (1994) *Princess Jazz and the Angels*, Mammoth
Nina Bawden (1995) *Granny the Pag*, Hamish Hamilton
Gillian Cross (1992) *The Great Elephant Chase*, Oxford
Berlie Doherty (1996) *Daughter of the Sea*, Puffin
Anne Fine (1992) *Flour Babies*, Puffin
Susan Fletcher (1998) *Shadow Spinner*, Bloomsbury.
Adele Geras (1998) *Silent Snow, Secret Snow*, Puffin
Pat Hutchins (1989) *Rats*, Bodley Head
Gene Kemp (1999) *The Hairy Hands*, Puffin
Geraldine McCaughrean (1997) *Forever X*, Oxford.
Mary Norton (1952) *The Borrowers*, Puffin
Jill Paton Walsh (1984) *Gaffer Sampson's Luck*, Puffin
Philip Pullman (1995) *The Firework Maker's Daughter*, Hippo
Robert Swindell (1977) *The Ice Palace*, Young Lions
Louis Sachar (2000) *Holes*, Bloomsbury
Robert Westall (1980) *Blitzcat*, Macmillan

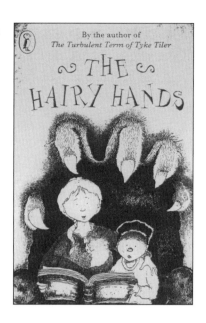

Chapter 6
A HUMANITIES FOCUS: THE RAINFOREST

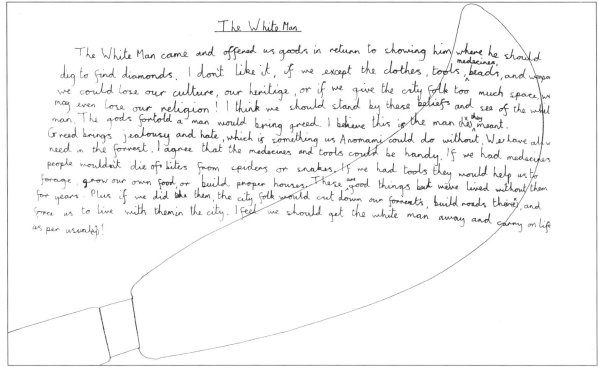

The White Man

The White Man came and offered us goods in return to showing him where he should dig to find diamonds. I don't like it, if we except the clothes, tools, medecines, beads, and weapons we could lose our culture, our heritage, or if we give the city folk too much space, we may even lose our religion! I think we should stand by these beliefs and see of the white man. The gods fortold a man would bring greed. I believe this is the man (they) meant. Greed brings jealousy and hate, which is something us Anomami could do without. We have all we need in the forrest. I agree that the medecines and tools could be handy. If we had medecines people wouldn't die of bites from spiders or snakes, If we had tools they would help us to forage, grow our own food, or build proper houses. These are good things but we've lived without them for years. Plus if we did take them, the city folk would cut down our forrent's, build roads there, and force us to live with them in the city. I feel we should get the white man away and carry on life as per usual!

Edward (aged 11)

Introduction

This drama is about the impact of a proposed mining development upon one of the indigenous tribes in the Amazon Rainforest; the Yanomami. The dramatic exploration provides a trigger to research and find out more about the complex issues around the destruction of the Rainforest. The information gathered is used in the drama, which in itself can prompt further investigation, so the drama feeds the research and vice versa.

The work involves the class in exploring life in the densely populated towns of the Amazon River Basin and examining the involvement of the World Bank in providing capital to develop open-cast mining in the Rainforest. The lives of the Yanomami, at peace with their neighbours and living in harmony with nature are then investigated, before a surveyor arrives to visit their community. The moral dilemma facing Brazil and the complex interplay between the environmental, social, political and economic forces is highlighted through this drama. A range of reference texts and resources are used, although these may be worked on more explicitly in time allocated to geography.

The two drama conventions highlighted in this chapter are **mantle of the expert** and **sound collage**. In the former, the children adopt roles, which allow them both to use and extend their geographical knowledge about the Rainforest. In the latter, the class are involved in making sounds to describe the environment and evoke atmosphere. Such sound collages encourage children to experiment with voice and body percussion and convey mood expressively.

Avoiding the children's suggestions and responses in order to follow the plan may mean that real opportunities for relevant learning are missed. A professional balance between teaching objectives and the children's interests is always required.

Teaching Objectives and Learning Areas

- Maintain and develop different roles during the drama (*the imagination*).
- Experiment with a range of verbal, gestural and movement portrayals to convey meaning (*the drama processes*).
- Develop knowledge and understanding of the complexity of environmental issues (*the content of the drama*).

Prior Experience and Materials

It is likely, given the growing concerns for the environment that the children will have some knowledge and opinion about the Rainforest. No specific prior study is necessary, although this extended project based drama will require textual resources and any previous work will feed into the drama.

- Relevant multimedia resources and a map of the world.
- Copies of the Yanomami role résumés.
- A blanket tied up with pots, pans, an axe, a bible and old clothes, a surveyor's hat.
- Large sheets of paper and pencils.

First Encounters: Creating the Drama Context

LIFE AND ASPIRATIONS IN THE FAVELAS

- Look at a map of the world with the class and locate South America, Brazil and the area of the Amazon River Basin. Provide some factual information about the numbers in the main towns like Rio de Janeiro and Sao Paulo, and the overcrowding in the favelas, the slums. Show some pictures and underline the need for better living conditions.

- Ask the children in groups to create freeze frames, photographs, which might have been taken by a European News Agency, showing the lives of the people in the favelas. These might highlight health, employment, living conditions, leisure time, education, or moments of pleasure or difficulty. Ask them to give their frames a title. Observe these together and ask some of the children what the thoughts or words of the person they are portraying might be, focus on the plight of these people.

- Ask the groups to create contrasting freeze frames of the affluent people in the cities in principally similar contexts.

- In pairs, suggest the children create a brief improvisation of situations in which members of the favelas meet the affluent people, e.g. a poor man cleaning and shining a businessman's shoes.

- Compose a shared letter from an altruistic citizen to a political representative in Sao Paulo calling for improvements in the lives and conditions of those who live in the favelas.

Conflicts and Tensions: Developing the Drama

MONEY FOR NATURAL RESOURCES

- In role as a politician, give an up-beat television news broadcast, proclaiming that a new era of increased prosperity is about to begin. The Brazilian Government has requested a large loan from The World Bank to invest in the development of an enormous open - cast mine in the Amazon

Rainforest. The minerals from this will generate the money to create the essential services, needed in the cities. Within the next few days officials of the World Bank will be arriving to begin discussions about the Government's proposals, so you are awaiting further developments.

• Suggest to the class that the deputy Prime Minister might call a meeting to consider the issues surrounding this enterprise. Discuss with them the kinds of people who might be invited. This should include representatives from scientific, industrial, financial, social and environmental interests. For example, town planners and housing officers who will need to plan for the communities of mine workers, mining officials excited by the opportunity, pharmaceutical researchers who intend to make use of the minerals for medicines, finance ministers, highway and transport officials, environmental ministers or lobby groups and so on. Exclude the Yanomami, although their interests might be represented by anthropologists. Write these up on the board, so the children can select a role to adopt at the meeting. Everyone should nominate his or her role so you can ensure a balance of representation through renegotiation if necessary. There will be duplication of some roles and groups may form. The children could find out more about their specialist focus through research at this point.

THE EXPERTS ARE DIVIDED

• Lay out the room formally and in role as the deputy Prime Minister, call all the experts together for a policy meeting to discuss the proposal prior to negotiations with the World Bank. Each child, or group if that is how interests are represented, should formally introduce themselves and their particular expertise. You will need to play devil's advocate in order to ensure all the different interests are represented, through questioning or offering alternatives and conflicting points of view. It is important that all the concerns represented by the children are considered. In role, state that it is a condition of the World Bank that it will not loan the money, unless all these issues have an equal and balanced airing.

• Close the meeting in role and summarise the arguments, suggesting that the Government intends to proceed to the next stage, and will be issuing a press statement and formally writing to the World Bank. Also, state that a preliminary survey with minimum disturbance to the Yanomami will go ahead in the proposed area. One or two people will carry this out, and the results from this survey will be used to make the final decision about whether the project proceeds.

• The Government's press statement or letter to the World Bank could be composed in written form, individually or through shared writing.

Research Work

The drama now moves to where the Yanomami live in the Rainforest. So it would be advisable to have an extended break from the drama to allow the children to become more detached from their previous roles, and to research the people of the Rainforest, their way of life and the environment in which they live. Literary texts can also help here, some are noted in the final section of this chapter.

THE YANO

THE IMPACT AREA: THE YANOMAMI AND THE RAINFOREST

• Show the class enlarged diagrams of the Yano, the open sided wood and palm branch building in which all the community live. Each family builds its own section around the fireplace where their hammocks are slung. Discuss this community home and the children's responses to it.

- Hand out the role resumés, extracts from the WWF resource 'The Yanomami', ensuring a spread of roles. Once they've been read, pair children up to share something of their different roles.

- Ask everyone to close their eyes and imagine they are lying in their hammock in the Yano looking into the forest around them. It is early in the morning, just as the sun is rising, the dew is still heavy and the birds and animals begin to fill the forest with their sounds. (A poem or extract from a text might enrich this visualisation). Ask the children to individually draw what they 'see' from their hammock, onto large pieces of paper.

- Suggest that small groups, compose a sound collage of that early morning which, somewhat like a piece of music, is interspersed with the silence of the forest. You might list together some of the possible sounds e.g. tree frogs and iguanas, macaws and toucans, the weather, the river and the rain. Encourage full use of voice and body percussion.

- Let each group perform their collage to evoke the environment, you might even extend this activity by orchestrating them together into a single cacophony which you conduct, with a formal beginning and ending. These can be extremely effective.

- To deepen the identification with the forest and the people, ask the children in groups to create a ritual of thanksgiving for the forest and the livelihood it provides. Discuss options with the class e.g. the ceremonial placing of honey or deer meat in a sacred place, the ritual burning of herbal medicine to acknowledge recovery from a spider's bite and so on. This will involve a ritualised slowing down, a sense of heightened significance. These could be improvisations with a narrator, or group rituals which are performed simultaneously or separately, but as the last concludes, narrate the people's return to the Yano, and the arrival of a white stranger.

A STRANGER AND A SHADOW ARRIVE

- As you narrate the arrival of the stranger, simultaneously assume the role of a surveyor perhaps with a hard hat or some piece of equipment, which signals the role. Carry with you a blanket tied up with items, which might have been carried by early traders when meeting native people eg. beads, pots and pans, old clothes, an axe and a bible. You may need to agree with the class that for the sake of the drama, English is spoken, since less experienced classes tend to parody speech through 'gobble-de-goop' pidgin, and this breaks up any gathering tension through embarrassment and laughter.

- Greet the Yanomami with non-threatening questions and open up your blanket. Explain you wish them no harm and ask for the chief, or leader in their group. Someone may be selected to take that role, or the group may just listen to you as you offer them gifts. Allow these to be passed around and talked about. During this, express an interest in the stones and minerals in the forest, and ask if the Yanomami have any knowledge of areas of these. Allow them to question you and be quite direct about your interest.

- Leave the Yano with at least the message that you will return to hear whether the people will guide you through the forest to sites rich in rocks and minerals. In this initial contact, the impression of genuineness, or trickery and exploitation, which is conveyed by your manner, will need to match whatever you feel is appropriate, in the light of the earlier government meeting.

- Either as a class or in family groups, or in a combination of both, discuss the situation and your views. The community will 'benefit' in some ways, if you tell the stranger about the mineral sites, and perhaps some of you have heard of other ways of life and are interested in them. Allow opinions to be expressed and differences aired.

- Return briefly in role as the surveyor to hear their decision and respond appropriately.

- Ask the children, either as a class or in pairs, to write the surveyor's report for the deputy PM. This will be considered at the next meeting of the policy group. If this is written in pairs, share extracts from the reports.

Resolutions: Drawing the Drama Together

THE GOVERNMENT THINK TANK RECONVENES

- In role as deputy PM, reconvene the policy meeting; remind the class of their previous roles and focus upon the issue of the desperate human needs in the favelas. This meeting will highlight the legitimate conflict of interests, the needs of different groups, environmental, human and financial perspectives, so tensions will inevitably arise. As deputy PM you'll need to make a decision about the proposal to develop open-cast mining in the Rainforest based upon the arguments offered.

- Ask groups to create freeze frames showing the consequence of the decision either for the Yanomami or the inhabitants of the favelas, ask groups to title these, and discuss the portrayals as a class.

- Suggest the children plan and produce a western TV documentary about this issue. This could be undertaken as a whole class with each group taking responsibility for one aspect of the situation or in small groups. Through this try to highlight the moral dilemma facing Brazil and the different views and interests involved.

- As you watch these documentaries, consider together other places in the world, which are being used for their natural resources and the possible or evident consequences.

Extension Activities

- Groups could turn their documentary, or section of one, into a television script for other groups to read, or the documentaries could be videoed for other classes to watch.

- Follow the life of the people of the Rainforest, the Yanomami, or Huaorani, many of whom remain there, but are obliged to come to terms with the advances of industrialisation.

- In drama, examine the assassination of 'Chico' Mendes the environmentalist, who in Brazil espoused the cause of the local forest rubber-tappers against the more wealthy ranchers, who want the forest cleared for their cattle.

- Balance the negative examples by studying successful cases, in which conflicting interests have been integrated, such as the growth of wild life around Cape Canaveral in Florida.

Resourcing Further Drama from the Humanities

The humanities are particularly rich in events and situations which can be explored imaginatively through drama, using factual information and prompting further research and investigation. First-hand accounts and writing produced by e.g. the early explorers, scientists, environmentalists, soldiers and so on are fertile resources for initiating and enriching joint humanities and drama projects. Newspaper reports, old or new, can also be used alongside other pictorial material, since the stories behind the images can be brought to life and the surrounding issues investigated.

In History, a wide variety of primary and secondary evidence can be integrated into drama to make the past more accessible to children and give them a richer understanding of historical events and awareness of others' cultural values. Drama enables children to make empathetic connections between the often abstract nature of primary sources and the real lives of men and women in the past, and it often generates as many questions as it does answers, so it provokes the need to find out.

By placing children within particular historical periods, it is possible to investigate a wealth of issues. For example, the meetings between Montezuma and the Aztecs, and why so few were able to subdue so many, the tensions for Elizabeth I as a Queen in a man's world or the working conditions of children and adults in Victorian England. Life and death in the trenches, and the evacuation of children to the countryside in the two World Wars could also be examined. Part of the planning process is completed through the selection of a historical focus, since the people, place and some of the predicaments already exist. The teacher's skill is in using drama conventions to develop an informed appreciation of the various viewpoints and opinions of those who lived in the past. Television programmes such as the BBC Landmarks Series can help as resources, as can historical novels or picture books. The latter frequently focus on how children behaved and were treated and this provides an accessible framework from which to examine the politics and living conditions of different periods of time. We recommend the following children's texts for supporting imaginative reconstruction in history.

The Romans
Tony Bradman (1989) *The Sandal*, Andersen
Rosemary Sutcliff (1996) *Song for a Dark Queen*, Red Fox

The Tudors
Michael Morpurgo (1990) *My friend Walter*, Heinemann
Penelope Lively (1972) *The Driftway*, Puffin

The Victorians
Berlie Doherty (1993) *Street Child*, Bodley Head
Dick King Smith (1993) *Lady Daisy*, Puffin

The 2nd World War II
Roberto Innocenti (1985) *Rose Blanche*, Jonathan Cape
Ann Turnbull (1998) *A Long Way Home*, Walker

The Greeks
Geraldine McCaughrean (1992) *The Orchard Book of Greek Myths* Orchard
Jane Yolen (1991) *Wings*, Harcourt Brace Jovanich

The Egyptians
Roy Gerrard (1994) *Croco' Nile*, Gollancz
Theresa Breslin (1999) *The Dream Master*, Corgi

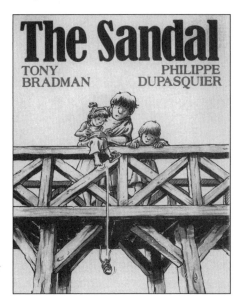

In Geography, a focus on a place often highlights the human and economic issues that surround it. Dramatic investigations can prompt further questions, enrich understanding of complexity and compromise and enable children to learn about geographical concerns in the imaginary context. For example, local environmental issues concerning new settlements such as the placement of new towns, the growth of suburbs, reduction of green belt land, new roads and shopping centres and so on can all lead to dramatic investigations, involving debates, discussions and persuasive writing. Equally, concerns related to places around the world can be examined through drama, for example the conservation of the tiger in India, the floods in Bangladesh, and family planning in China. Other environmental issues such as pollution, erosion and conservation concerns can also be investigated through drama, in a focus on rivers or through examining how the land is used. Fictional picture texts are often useful resources for such investigations, as these can guide the drama. We recommend the following:

Brian Patten (1993) *The Magic Bicycle*, Walker
Eljay Yildrim (1997) *Aunty Dot's Incredible Adventure Atlas*, Collins
Lynne Cherry (1990) *The Great Kapok Tree: A Tale of the Amazon Rain Forest*, Harcourt Brace
Florence Heide and Judith Gilliland (1991) *The Day of Ahmed's Secret*, Gollancz (Egypt)
Susan Jeffers (1991) *Brother Eagle, Sister Sky: A Message from Chief Seattle*, Dial
Juliet and Charles Snape (1989) *Giant*, Walker

A Hunter

I lie in my hammock enjoying the peace of the morning when suddenly the peace is shattered by the sound of a dog fight. The winner of the fight is a bewitched dog who is really the spirit of another warrior, whom I once offended and who has returned to annoy me and remind me of my guilt. Although we burn the possessions of the dead, their spirits live on and even the shaman can do nothing to help.

After an early morning game with my son I join my other two children at the hearth where they are quietly drinking plantain soup. My brothers-in-law have hearths close by and everyone shares the task of feeding the family. The children finish their soup and run off to play at hunting while I get ready to go on a real hunt. I usually carry three arrows and spare arrow heads made of different materials for different prey. My bow is made of a peach palm and strung with a plant fibre from my garden. We have now lived at this yano for so long it is quite difficult to find enough animals to hunt and soon I must speak to my father-in-law about moving to a new site. I leave the yano and enter the dark forest. Quite soon my eyes get used to the darkness and after quite a search a capuchin monkey appears. Quietly I prepare my arrow head and fire - got him! Further on I find signs of a peccary, and smell the scent. I fire but this arrow is just to slow him down and not to kill him. I chase him for some way and at last he falls down and I finish him off. These will make fine offerings for my family today. Tomorrow, perhaps, by brother-in-law will hunt and I can rest.

A Woman

I climb down from my hammock. My daughter, who is seven, is getting up too. She usually helps me with my jobs in the morning or when I need her to, otherwise she will spend the day playing with other girls around the yano. It will not be very many years now before she will marry and have children of her own. My first job is to sweep the hearth and tend to the fire which is kept burning all the time. I got up several times last night to poke the  ashes for a little more warmth, as it is quite cold just before dawn. We take any rubbish from the hearth to a dump at the edge of the forest. Next, I must prepare our meal. There is some meat left from yesterday's catch still smoking on the fire and I set some bananas to bake on the cinders at the edge of it. We drink banana mash after the meal.

Next we go down to the river to collect water for the day. I have a metal pot which we managed to get by trading with another yano. That job done, I call my daughter and we go back to the river with some of the other women and girls to bathe. The river is deep and fast-running at this time of year so we must stand at the very edge of it. I admire another woman's body paint; she has some beautiful red patterns on her. The red dye is made from a plant called urucu. We either smear the seeds straight onto our skin or we heat them in a pot with some water and make a paste, which we roll into balls. We also use charcoal and a black dye made from the fruit of the genipapo tree, but that is only for feasts. We use red for everyday wear. Later I lie in my hammock and catch up with some of the news in the yano. We talk about the feast that is going to take place soon, at the end of the rainy season. It is a funerary feast to dispose of the ashes of someone who died in our yano.

A Child

Today is like most other days and I shall spend it playing with my friends in the yano. One of our favourite games is hunting and I have my own small sized bow and arrow. Sometimes we shoot the lizards which scuttle across our hearth, we cook them over the fire. They are not very nice to eat but catching them is very good for improving my aim with the bow. When I am older I shall make myself a big bow and arrows and go hunting in the forest with my brothers. Sometimes we boys have mock fights with the girls and have to escape by climbing up the tall poles of the yano. From the top of my pole I can see a group of visitors coming through the trees. I always like to see new people but they want to talk business with the elders and look rather serious.

I go over to where my sister is helping with the making of a new hammock. A wooden frame has been made and a very long strand of cotton has been wound round and round the frame. My sister is weaving in cross pieces which she ties with knots to keep them in place. Our hammocks are the most important things we have, they can be made just of long strips of liana knotted together at the ends, but the cotton ones are more comfortable. My sister is nearly twelve and is always taking a lot of trouble to make herself look nice for her husband.

A Shaman

My initiation lasted for eight days and I had to learn all sorts of secrets like the taking of yakoana which is made from the bark of a particular tree. This is very dangerous and makes shamans do special dances and gives us strange dreams. It also gives us the ability to see and talk to the evil spirits and to call on our own good spirits or hekura which are shaped like humans, animals or plants. This morning I have some important work to do, a boy is ill and his parents have asked me to cure him. I shall be trying to free him of the evil spirits or 'yai' which have crawled into his body. Yai are

the spirits or ghosts of animals killed by Yanomami hunters which come back to get their revenge by making people ill. We believe that good and bad spirits are around us all the time, in the sky, the forest, - everywhere. Ordinary people can't see them - but then you can't see the wind, but you know it is there. I can see spirits when I am in a special trance and that is why I am called an 'Explorer of the Spirit World'.

Severiano is nine years old - like me he has a Spanish name, given to us by the missionaries some years ago. The first thing I do is to make friends with my patient, so we sit talking and making jokes, picking the lice from each other's hair. This is good sign that he trusts me. Several villagers have arrived to watch and I begin by taking some yakoana. I start my dance, lift the boy into the air, hug him and put him down. I do this for some time. After a while I begin to see the ugly 'yai', the evil spirits in his head. They look like coloured insects with many legs. I introduce myself and my hekura spirits and after some arguing I ask them to leave. Some jump out through his ear and rush off into the forest, but one refuses. Eventually, after much dancing and chanting this yai decides to leave. I call one of my hekura spirits -a frog - to pour water over the boy and then I give him back to his mother.

Chapter 7
A Personal and
Social Issue
DOWN THE ARCADES

> Dear Dean,
>
> I feel so guilty and Horrible but its for your own good Dean. listen I've been hard on you, but its for youre own good. if this doesnt work you'll have to go to boarding school, or you'll end up a real criminal and I dont wont that to happen, youre going to have to change your friends, that Crowd are wasters, drinking and Smoking and wasting their money on the machines. Please Dean Pull your Socks up and dont be stupid — I thought that you were going to be Perfect when you were born but I was wong, try and Prove me wright
>
> from
> Dad x
>
> PS Rember this is for your own good

Callum (aged 10)

Introduction

The source of this drama is a personal and social issue, the obsessive nature of habits and gambling on arcade slot machines. This work was first undertaken in response to a class of pupils who, at the close of an earlier drama about a missing classmate, all showed in their separate improvisations, that the truant had gone to the amusement arcade to play on the slot machines. A discussion followed, demonstrating their knowledge and enthusiasm for the temptations of the arcades, so this focus was selected for a dramatic exploration. In working with this theme, the teacher and the class devised a drama that explored the possible consequences of persistent gambling.

The overarching narrative which frames this drama is simply that a family, working hard to save money, find that some of their savings have disappeared. The parents know it must be one of their children and try to handle it themselves, but the problem persists, and eventually they seek 'outside support'. In some classes this has involved the welfare, in others the police, while in still others, members of the extended family have met to resolve the problem. In this drama, the fictional boy is named Dean. Be sure to rename him if you have anyone in your class with that name.

The drama conventions highlighted in this chapter are **forum theatre** and **writing in role**. In the former, a small group act out a scene in the drama for the rest of the class to observe. The observers or the actors can stop the action at any point and make suggestions about how it might develop or ask for a replay with particular changes. The resultant theatre is therefore produced through the forum of the class, all of whom can contribute ideas to it. The writing in role in this drama is undertaken at the end from a number of different viewpoints. This helps the children to reflect upon their drama and may deepen their response to it. The different genres and registers chosen make interesting comparisons since they all emerge from the same drama situation.

Avoiding the children's suggestions and responses in order to follow the plan may mean that real opportunities for relevant learning are missed. A professional balance between teaching objectives and children's interests is always required.

Teaching Objectives and Learning Areas

- Inform and develop their own moral values (*personal and social skills*).
- develop insight and empathy through writing in role (*language*).
- make connections between the drama and the real world (*reflection*).

Prior Experience and Materials

No particular experience is necessary, although this work would fit well into a personal and social education focus.

- Paper and pencils for everyone
- Social work report sheets (optional)

First Encounters: Creating the Drama Context

OUR HABITS

- Begin by sharing some of your own patterns of living or habitual behaviours, such as Saturday supermarket shopping, a regular Sunday afternoon walk, your daily newspaper and so on. Then prompt discussion about the children's patterns of behaviour or frequent use of particular expressions e.g. "I say well wicked or cool dude all the time", "I bite my nails", other examples may involve patterns of eating, or particular TV watching, purchasing a regular comic or specific drinks, buying lottery tickets and so on.

- Discuss which habits would be the hardest to give up, and which might have implications if you were hooked upon them e.g. a particular programme choice dominating others' viewing or the unhealthy consequences of too much chocolate and too many chips. Ponder together on how such patterns of behaviour become obsessive.

- Explain that the drama is going to focus on one family and the consequences of a habit which turned into an obsession. Tell them that the Thurston family made up of a mum, dad, and a brother and sister (of an age relevant to your class) had been saving for weeks for a decent day out. They'd got £51 so far in a tin and hadn't yet decided where to go for the special day trip. Brainstorm possible ideas for the outing, where would your class choose to go?

- Explain that members of the family occasionally dreamt of their perfect day out. Ask groups to show a freeze frame of one member of the family's dream. Watch these together.

- Suggest the class improvise the family's discussion about where to go, in the same small groups. Listen to a few brief snippets of these.

Conflicts and Tensions: Developing the Drama

MONEY IS MISSING

- Ask the children to watch you in role as mum, sometime the next day. Briefly mime e.g. vacuuming, making a coffee and then going to count the money in the tin. Show your surprise at the amount of money and then ring your husband, explaining in a panic that some of the savings are missing.

- Ask for a volunteer to be dad and choose someone you know can maintain the role, or suggest the whole class take up dad's role on the other end of the phone. Whichever option, allow the class to discuss what dad might feel or say, before you return to your role as mum.

- In role as mum, start the telephone conversation again by counting the money and ringing your husband. Share your suspicion that your son has returned to his habit of spending money on the slot machines. Build upon this fear by recalling his recent Saturday absences, and the missing fishing rod that disappeared a while ago. Dean had never liked fishing, so what had happened to the rod? In the conversation with the father, take up a contrasting position to him and maintain your concerns. Finish the conversation flustered and worried.

- Ask the class what they think the mother would do? Suggestions have included, she'd ring a friend, or her mother, her sister or the head teacher, she'd search the children's bedrooms, count the money again or march down to the school to confront her son. Agree upon one line of action, and in pairs briefly improvise the conversation or phone-call and listen to snippets of these.

- As yourself, discuss with the class the evidence that the son has taken the money, is it merely circumstantial evidence based upon on his past track record and fascination with slot machines and the amusement arcades? What are the implications for the parents in the light of this 'evidence'?

DOWN THE ARCADES

- Tell the class that even as mum was on the phone, her son was truanting from school and going down to the local amusement arcade. Discuss their favourite arcade games, eg. simulators, slot machines, video games, 'claws to catch a toy', and so on and where they have played such games.

- Ask everyone to take up the role of people in the amusement arcade that day. Improvise this for a short time and then freeze the action, and walk around touching individuals on the shoulder asking them to think out loud, and express their thoughts, about being there.

- Remind the class that these games clearly attract Dean to spend his money, and discuss briefly what they think he likes about them.

- Ask the children to work in small groups and physically create the shape of one of the machines with their bodies. When these have been made, suggest they arrange the machines in rows, back to back as they would find in arcades.

- Explain that one child in role as Dean, will walk up and down the rows of machines listening to their words of temptation. If he is persuaded by their 'sales-pitch' he may stop and have a go on the game before he walks on. Give the groups time to invent their 'sales-speak' and ask the pairs to speak mechanically or robotically as the machine tempting the boy to play on them.

- Let Dean walk around the amusement arcade and respond to the temptations. When he has travelled the rows, ask him to tell the class, what he feels about the arcades and how he feels about the behaviour he is suspected of, that is taking his parents' money and spending it on the machines.

THE PROBLEM PERSISTS - SOMETHING MUST BE DONE

- Narrate the passage of time with the family's day out being 'put-off', comment that the money was never found, and both children denied taking it. Several weeks later, however first mum and then dad found money missing from their wallets, and then the savings tin was depleted once more. The headteacher had reported Dean's increased truancy, and something had to be done.

- Ask the class to discuss the problem in pairs as mum and dad. What are the various options open to them, who else could get involved and how might they help?

- Either listen to snippets or ask the class to share the parents' ideas about what might be done to resolve the family's problem. Agree a way forward and then establish a piece of forum theatre based on their plan. This has included an extended family conference, a meeting at the school, and the involvement of the welfare office. The last suggestion is detailed here, but the same structure can be paralleled in the other contexts if they are chosen.

- Ask for volunteers to take the roles of Dean's parents and one or two welfare officers. You could take on the challenging role of Dean or request a volunteer. Give this small group some time to discuss how they are going to construct this interview/case conference in front of the class.

- Whilst this is going on, ask the advice of the rest of the class about how to set up the room. Organise the space for the interview accordingly.

- Suggest that the rest of the class take up roles as social workers in training and that they are able to watch the interview with the juvenile, his parents and the welfare officer(s), through a one-way mirror. Ask them to listen carefully, as they'll be required to make recommendations after the conference about how the family can resolve their problems. If you are not Dean you may like to be another welfare officer, perhaps a junior one, so the group take responsibility for their work, but you can have a voice in the meeting if necessary.

- Let the forum theatre begin, and depending on their experience of this convention, either allow the class to stop the action, comment and suggest alternative behaviours to the actors, or ask the class to watch and inform them that you'll interrupt the conference.

- If you interrupt the action, comment on the proceedings so far, and then allot each of the actors one group of observers whom they can turn to for advice. Explain the interview will be revisited and that the actors must try to use the various angles and ideas offered. The group are expected to make suggestions eg. one group will seek to help Dean by offering alternative ideas, possible bargaining points or words and phrases which he might employ in the interview.

- Re-establish the forum theatre, either beginning again or continuing from where it had reached. Remind the actors to use the advice they have been given.

Resolutions: Drawing the Drama Together

RECOMMENDATIONS AND RESULTS

- When the interview has been concluded, allow the actors a few moments to comment on the conference from their point of view.

- Provide the trainee social workers, the bulk of the class, with forms to record a summary of the problem and their recommendations. The family and the welfare officers can make their own choices about the audience, form and purpose of their writing. You could mention letters, diaries, and case reports if you want, but let them choose. Join the class in this writing in role, making your own choice also.

- This writing in role will need peace and quiet and a reasonable length of time. Use the space available and avoid moving furniture around at this moment.

- Offer the children the opportunity to read a section of their writing to the class. Discuss the issues raised and whether they think the problem was solved.

- Ask groups to show a flashforward freeze frame, which in some way reflects the boy's life ten years later. Suggest each group adds a title to their representation.

- Look at these, and discuss what they imply about the boy, his character and the nature of obsessive habits. Extend this discussion to include their own and others' habits and the lessons possible to learn from this drama.

CONFIDENTIAL REPORT
No :25389/14.7.00

Case study summary:

Name : Dean Thurston. Regular 'borrowing' of family money. Skips school (St. Mathews) and spends time in the Arcades. Parents are worried, father is furious. The family came for advice.

Recommendations:

As a fellow social worker I recommend that Dean should be grounded for at least a month. But do not ground him for much longer or he may turn against his family. He should pay the money back to teach him a lesson. Also the family should not keep large sums of money at home, they should use a bank.

When he's paid it back they should all go on the day trip together, it will be good for them. I'm concerned this addiction does not develop further, he must be encouraged to find other interests, can he start a new hobby?

Dear Mr and Mrs Thurston

It was good to meet you on thursday I trust our meeting helped. I have talked to our staff and have some more suggestions for you. Do not tell your parents about this promblem as it may afect them badly. It is harder when you are old to hear about the young. Right to Dean because sometimes it easyer to write to them than to face a person. In your letter you must try to explane to him that grounding him will help him. Some people who hang around the Arcades are hooked, if he keeps this up he'll be in debt, when he's older.

Tell him not to be threatened by any one down the Arcades whatever. He can make his own mind up and make his own choices.

I trust this helps you

your sencirly

John Barnem
Senior social worker

Neil (aged 10)

John (aged 10)

Extension Activities

- Produce emotions graphs from Dean's perspective about significant events in the drama and then write a retrospective entry in Dean's diary about one of these. Discuss what this reveals about his perspective and character.

- As a personal and social education focus, collect and discuss reports and newspaper articles on addictive habits and behaviour. Draw parallels and focus on the consequences of these habits for the individuals, their families and friends.

- In circle time, explore some of the issues raised in the drama. These may include peer pressure, obsessive habits, truancy, compulsions, responsibility for one's own behaviour, and empathy with others.

Resourcing Further Drama from Personal and Social Issues

Classroom drama frequently examines difficult aspects of human living and can help to highlight the complexity of moral issues and different individual's values and perspectives as well as those of society at large. Since drama is the art form of social encounters, it always uses personal and social skills and explores moral concerns, but this is often an implicit, rather than an explicit focus in drama. However children can develop self-confidence, self-esteem, and their self-image through drama as well as their ability to empathise with others. It is clear therefore, that drama can promote personal and social education and contribute to the development of citizenship as well as handle sensitive issues. Indeed, in drama, children often have to act collectively rather than in their own interests, negotiating and taking decisions together. In addition, drama is particularly good for developing affective learning, for exploring and presenting information in the context of people's lives rather than as abstract factual information.

In this drama about the temptations of the arcades, the children's interest in and enthusiasm for this particular pastime was used as the reason for developing a drama around the possible consequences of this habit. Tuning into children's interests and taking these as a theme and resource for drama is a powerful way of responding to personal and social issues relevant to the class. Teachers can plan drama around almost any aspect of the PSHE curriculum and examine these issues in relation to a fictional family or other group facing the challenges involved. The range of perspectives explored, the reasons for the behaviour, and the consequences of it, as well as the coping strategies employed can all be investigated. Chapter 15 responds to some teachers' concerns about particularly sensitive issues, but any number can be explored safely in drama, for example loss, relationships, prejudice, HIV/Aids, bullying and substance use and abuse.

Both fiction and non fiction texts can be useful in resourcing such drama, many are noted as resources in other chapters based on novels, newspaper extracts or picture books.

We also recommend:

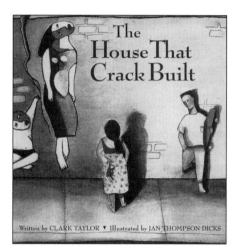

Margaret Wild (1999) *Jenny Angel*, Viking (death and loss)
Laurence Anholt (1995) *The Magpie Song*, Heinemann (death and loss)
Clark Taylor (1992) *The House that Crack Built*, Chronicle (drugs)
Caroline Binch (1998) *Since Dad left*, Frances Lincoln (divorce)
Jane Yolen (1992) *Encounter*, Haircourt Brace Jovanovich (prejudice)
Maurice Gleitzman (1989) *Two weeks with the Queen*, Puffin (HIV, sexuality, bereavement)

Chapter 8
A FAITH TALE: A BABY IN THE BULLRUSHES

> *It's dark. I hear houses being ripped apart and babies screaming. I can't help myself. I start to cry.*
>
> *Just then I hear soldiers asking my mother where I am. She said I was not here. "You lie!" said the soldier.*

Rheanna (aged 10)

Introduction

This drama is based upon the persecution of the Israelites in Egypt, as it is found in The Bible, Exodus 1 and 2. In particular the story of the new-born Moses, who is placed in a basket and hidden in the bullrushes by the river Nile to avoid being butchered by the Pharaoh's soldiers. The Bible passage is read at the end of the drama, partly for its content and partly for the poetry and impact of the words themselves.

The tale tells how the Egyptian Pharaoh at that time developed a sense of insecurity, amounting to paranoia over the number of Israelites in his land. Concerned lest they should join his enemies or plot against him, he set them to work as slaves helping to build great new cities. But the people of Israel still flourished, so to reduce their numbers, the Pharaoh ordered that the Hebrew midwives should kill all the new-born baby boys. But the fearful midwives tricked the Pharaoh, who was so enraged, that he commanded every baby boy be drowned in the Nile. Jochebed and Amram, an Israelite couple, fearful of their new baby's safety, made a cradle from the river weeds and placed their son, in it. They took him down to the bank of the great river Nile and left him there, trusting that he would survive the dangers and that God would care for him.

The drama conventions highlighted here are **ritual** and **teacher in role**. In the former, the children are part of an event, which uses ritualised speech and movement to heighten the experience and to slow down the action. In the latter, teacher in role is used to influence events from within the situation and to challenge the children's thinking. Out of role, the teacher also gives contextual information in the drama, and helps the class reflect upon the emerging issues.

Avoiding the children's suggestions and responses in order to follow the plan may mean that real opportunities for relevant learning are missed. A professional balance between teaching objectives and children's interests is always required.

Teaching Objectives and Learning Areas
- Examine the social and moral issues in the drama (*personal and social skills*).
- Widen the range of verbal, gestural, and movement skills employed (*the drama process*).
- Expand upon and explore their knowledge of the persecution of the Israelites (*the content of the drama*).

Prior Experience and Materials

No prior knowledge of the story is necessary, but it would sit well within a focus on ancient Egypt. If the class have heard the story of Moses before, you might draw attention to this and explain that you are going to investigate some of the issues which surround the tale and the events leading up to his discovery in the bullrushes. Alternatively, you could simply undertake the drama and allow the class to make connections as it unfolds.

- A clipboard and paper.
- A basket and a cloth to swaddle an imaginary infant.
- A Bible.
- Paper and pencils for everyone.

First Encounters: Creating the Drama Context

FARMING LIFE IN ANCIENT EGYPT

- Ask the children to think of the kinds of jobs people in an Egyptian farming community would do, discuss both livestock and arable farming. Consider the hardships and difficulties farmers from this time might have faced, for instance, swarms of locusts.

- Ask them to spread out in the space available and individually choose a job and mime it. Circulate, asking individuals to say out loud what it is they are doing, and encourage a few to elaborate by asking questions e.g. how are you going to keep the birds from eating your seed?

- In small groups, create two contrasting freeze-frames of farmers in times of plenty and of difficulty, e.g. with high crop yields or when drought or disease beset their harvest.

HARSH TREATMENT FOR THE ISRAELITES

- Ask the class to mime the jobs they selected as you briefly narrate a typical working day for the Israelites labouring in the fields of the Pharaoh. Conclude this by introducing, and taking on the role of an Egyptian foreman arriving in the fields, to demand the 'first fruits' of the harvest, as payment to the Pharaoh for the use of his land. Make it clear that the Israelites are slaves and behave in a direct almost brutal manner with them. This role indirectly embodies a great deal about the power and authority system, and reflects how the Egyptians viewed the Israelites.

- Sit down at a table with your clipboard and call for everyone to bring forward their 'first fruits' tax payment. If your class need some thinking time, ask them to sit in family groups to decide what it is that they are going to give the Pharaoh.

- Call pairs to come up to you to give their 'first fruits', demand their names and those of their family. Write all this down on your clipboard. It is possible that at this juncture some children will take up their roles as Israelite peasants and begin to object and grumble about the conditions they labour in. If so, respond in role appropriately to any such behaviour.

- In pairs or small groups allows them to discuss their plight and their feelings, in the short break they are allowed to take at midday.

- During this small group discussion, narrate that not all the 'first fruits' were given, some were kept back and hidden, ask the children to decide if they did this, what they held back and why.

- Make a circle and place an empty chair in the middle, inviting the children to come forward to the chair to give 'witness' to the rest of the class, as to what they gave and what they withheld and why.

- Conclude this section by discussing what the Israelites might have found hard to give up. Extend this to the children themselves, within their own families – what possessions would they be loathe to give up to others?

THE PHARAOH IS AFRAID

- Introduce the Pharaoh, the Egyptian King, via a brief narration and then move into role as him, looking out of his palace and seeing Israelites everywhere at work in the fields. Your voice and movement need to express agitation, rising to extremes: *'Why are they all about me? I can't trust them! They will take it all, what will happen to me and my people?'*

- Then step back into narration, explaining that the Pharaoh was troubled with nightmares in which he felt the Israelites were threatening him, for he was afraid of their numbers and thought they might plot against him.

- Ask the class to enact one of his troublesome dreams, by going to the edge of the space and then slowly advancing upon, you, the Pharaoh, asleep in the centre of the room on a chair. Narrate this sequence, and rather in the vein of the old playground game Grandmother's Footsteps, when The Pharaoh's eyes are open, the children, (the Israelite spirits in his mind), freeze and call out their grievances and worries as Israelites. The Pharaoh, in turn can call out in the terror of his nightmare all the guilty fears he has about these people. Just before they finally reach you, awake and leap up, calling out for your Chief Ministers in alarm and anger.

- Move away to a clear space and be seen to calm down, take up a more sinister and calculating manner and call out again for your Chief Ministers.

Conflicts and Tensions: Developing the Drama

THE PHARAOH BEGINS TO PLOT

- Maintaining the same momentum, look towards two or three children, who from your experience have the confidence and personality to accept the roles of your Ministers. Alternatively, you could have asked them earlier in the drama, and have them nearby you throughout the dream sequence.

- Call them to you, using 'Egyptian' names e.g. Ahmed or Mustafa, and speak to them about the Israelites, conclude by ordering them to go into the Israelite village and bring back their midwives. Say that there are some important matters you need to consult them about, but be vague, and perhaps include an air of secrecy about the matter. All this should be overheard by the rest of the class

> Move as fast as you can.
> The soldiers are getting closer every second,
> Run and do not come back!

> WARNING!!
> If the pharaoh asks you to come to the palace,
> and asks you if you have any boys under the age of 5, say NO!
> If you say yes, the soldiers will surely come and kill them!
> He did it in our village, he might do it in yours.

- Send off the children in role as your Ministers, to talk to the rest of the class who have the roles of the Israelites, in order to identify who their midwives are. There may or may not be discussion amongst them as to whether anyone should co-operate. The rest of the class will have to sort out their roles, and if they refuse to send midwives, insist that the elders are brought before you. This meeting with the midwives, or elders, should be held with a formality bordering upon ritual.

> You have time to escape, run!
> The soldiers are coming to kill your children.
> You must leave now!
> Leave all your possessions behind,
> just get out of here!

- Speak to the Israelite midwives/elders in flattering terms, asking about themselves, their families and their people.

(10 and 11 Year Olds)

63

This role-play needs to be seen by the rest of the class and at its conclusion, ask them to return to their village and find out who has recently had a birth in the family, and if any of these babies were boys. If so they must return to you with the details. Should they be suspicious, offer them money and rewards, and suggest they are carrying out this survey for the benefit of all. Dismiss the midwives very formally, but with thanks.

- These children in role as midwives must now return to the Israelite village to find out the information, or not, according to the feelings the children have about the whole situation. There are at least two ways this can be achieved: either in small family groups who listen to what is being asked of them, and talk over what they will do, or the whole class can meet as the villagers and decide what to do. These are crucial discussions, which allow the children the time to think, so only take part in these discussions yourself, if you wish to play devils' advocate and stimulate thought.

THE MASSACRE

- In role as the Pharaoh, call the midwives back to you to give you the information you need. If they are not prepared to tell you or seek to ask you questions, 'fob' them off and dismiss them quickly. As soon as they have left, summon your Chief Ministers, and instruct them to inform all the Egyptian soldiers to search out every baby boy in the Israelite villages and drown them in the River Nile. The girls may be spared, but every Hebrew son is to perish.

- Suggest that as soon as this massacre began, the Israelite villagers started trying to escape or hide their babies. In groups let the children plan their family's response to this appalling situation. Share their ideas as a class.

- Ask the groups to make freeze-frames, which show the Israelites homes being searched, and the children in hiding.

- Ask each group to give their depiction a title and observe each of these as a class.

- Suggest some Israelites wrote notes in hiding or diary entries which reflected their thoughts and fears as they awaited the soldiers' arrival.

> I cannot tell you where we are. But I have taken Thoremu to the best hiding place there is. Thoremu thinks its just a game. I told him it is and we have to be quiet or else they will find us. We have to go now. The soldiers are getting closer every minute

Kusal (aged 11)

> What is going to happen to me? I hear footsteps outside. I want to see them. But Mama says don't come out. I ask why, she said they would kill you. Who are the pharaoh's soldiers? Who ever reads this show it to my Mama. It's freezing down here.

Danielle (aged 10)

> I don't know what was happening. My Mum just told us to, "Hurry, and get into the cellar as fast as possible." Me and my brothers were scared stiff as we could hear the soldiers getting closer to the house.

Liam (aged 10)

Resolutions: Drawing the Drama Together

THE FAREWELL

- Narrate slowly how the villagers hid their children (use their ideas) and how one mother, Jochebed, wrapped up her baby and placed him in a basket she'd woven with her own hands. Whilst you do this, ritually retrieve your basket from wherever you have kept it out of sight.

- Make a circle with the children, with you holding the basket. Put the basket on the floor in front of you and either mime placing a baby in it, or fold up the cloth and place it in, then slowly lift the basket up, all the time looking at your 'baby'. Allow time for the significance of this event to take hold in silence.

- Narrate that Jochebed, placed one special keepsake in the basket with her baby, in the hope that her son would survive, to help him through his life ahead. Take the basket into the centre of the circle and say a few farewell words and leave your 'gift', e.g. *'I leave you a lock of my hair, and hope one day we will meet again'*. Return slowly to your place in the circle. Then turn to the child next to you, and with the same tone of voice, ask them what they left with their child as they said goodbye, and pushed the basket out into the current of the river. Gesture towards the basket in the centre of the circle, inviting this child to go forward and leave their imaginary object and say farewell. Continue around the circle in a ritualised manner allowing each child who wishes to, to say its farewells. Alternatively, you could pass the basket to the child next to you, saying similar words, and asking him/her to take a turn of farewell and pass it on. Time may be needed for the children to gather their thoughts but try to keep the reflective atmosphere and concentration involved in the ritual.

- Whilst everyone is still in the circle read the passages from Exodus 1 and 2 in the Bible, which tell of the Israelites' persecution, and end with Pharaoh's daughter rescuing Moses from the river. Read from an actual Bible and give copies to the class.

- Conclude with everyone gathered around you to discuss the drama and their feelings about the story. Focus on Moses' mother's act of giving up her son in the basket, and reflect upon how sacrifice is sometimes necessary, but that it is something that can only be chosen and never imposed. Consider the moral issues involved when we are confronted with such decisions, and the faith that she showed in this tale.

- Specifically discuss what the children felt during the slow ritual farewell, did the convention evoke a different sense of the occasion. If so, how did it affect this? Contrast this with the Pharaoh's ritualised dream.

- Ask the class in groups to discuss parallel situations in the world and make a freeze-frame depicting a situation of persecution, either in the past or in the 21st Century. Observe these together.

Extension Activities

- Using this faith tale as a springboard, find out more about other historical or contemporary examples of prejudice, persecution, and injustice. Build on the knowledge reflected in the final freeze-frames.

- Study more of the life of Moses, how God spoke to him in the burning bush and how Moses led the Israelites out of Egypt and received the Ten Commandments on Mount Sinai.

Resourcing Further Drama from Faith Tales

The moral dilemmas and social issues, which permeate faith tales, make them very appropriate resources for drama. Such tales examine values and explore fundamental human and religious concepts, such as love, hope and redemption as well as those of good and evil, and also point up the uniqueness of individuals. Through dramatic explorations of faith tales, children can deepen their understanding of particular religions and the significant people in them. Extracts from the tale can be read aloud before, during, or after the drama and can be studied through comparison with the drama. The themes underpinning the tale can be prefigured and examined in drama, so through working in analogy, the theme is explored through a parallel, perhaps more contemporary situation. Later, connections can be made between that analogy and the faith tale. Clearly a wide range of secular texts can be used to examine key religious concepts, but faith tale collections are also useful, in particular we recommend:

Elizabeth Breuilly and Sandra Palmer (1993) *A Tapestry of Tales*, Collins Educational.
This useful collection provides brief retellings of a wide range of traditional stories. These include tales about how life began, about the wise and the foolish and about money, as well as tales from the six major world religions recognised in the NC. Some included are legendary, while other have a historical basis of some kind.

Margaret Mayo and Louise Brierley (1995) *The Orchard Book of Creation Stories*, Orchard.

Madhur Jaffrey (1985) *Seasons of Splendour*, Puffin.

Andrew Wood (1996) *Creation Stories*, The Education TV Company.

The series *Tales of Heaven and Earth*, Moonlight.

The series *Stories from World Religions*, Heinemann.

Exodus 1 v 8 - 22

Now there arose a new king over Egypt, who did not know Joseph. And he said to his people, 'Behold the people of Israel are too many and too mighty for us. Come, let us deal shrewdly, lest they multiply, and if war befall us, they join our enemies and fight against us and escape from the land.' Therefore they set taskmasters over them to afflict them with heavy burdens; and they built for Pharaoh stone cities, Pithom and Raam'ses. But the more they were oppressed, the more they multiplied and the more they spread abroad. And the Egyptians were in dread of the people of Israel. So they made the people of Israel serve with rigour, and made their lives bitter with hard service in mortar and brick, and in all kinds of work in the field; in all their work they made them serve with rigour.

Then the king of Egypt said to the Hebrew midwives, one of whom was named Shiph'rah and the other Pu'ah, 'When you serve as a midwife to the Hebrew women, and see them upon the birthstool, if it is a son, you shall kill him; but if it is a daughter, she shall live'. But the midwives feared God, and did not do as the king of Egypt commanded them, but let the male children live. So the king of Egypt called the midwives, and said to them, 'Why have you done this, and let the male children live?' The midwives said to Pharaoh, 'Because the Hebrew women are not like the Egyptian women; for they are vigorous and are delivered before the midwife comes to them'. So God dealt well with the midwives; and the people multiplied and grew very strong. And because the midwives feared God, he gave them families. Then Pharaoh commanded all his people, 'Every son that is born to the Hebrews, you shall cast into the Nile, but you shall let every daughter live.'

Exodus 2 v 1 - 10

Now a man from the house of Levi went and took as his wife a daughter of Levi. The woman conceived and bore a son; and when she saw that he was a goodly child, she hid him three months. And when she could hide him no longer, she took for him a basket made of bullrushes, and daubed it with bitumen and pitch; and she put the child in it and placed it among the reeds at the river's brink. And his sister stood at a distance to know what would be done to him.

Now the daughter of Pharaoh came down to bathe at the River; she saw the basket among the reeds and sent her maid to fetch it. When she opened it she saw the child; and lo, the babe was crying. She took pity on him and said 'This is one of the Hebrews' children'. Then his sister said to Pharaoh's daughter, 'Shall I go and call you a nurse you a Hebrew woman to nurse the child for you?' And Pharaoh's daughter, said to her, 'Go'. So the girl went and called the child's mother. And Pharaoh's daughter said to her, 'Take this child away, and nurse him for me and I will give you wages'. So the woman took the child and nursed him. And the child grew, and she brought him to Pharaoh's daughter, and he became her son; and she named him Moses, 'Because I drew him out of the water.'

(Revised Standard Version)

Chapter 9

A PICTURE: AND WHEN DID YOU LAST SEE YOUR FATHER? BY WILLIAM YEAMES

Introduction

This drama is based upon the famous Victorian painting by William Frederick Yeames (1835 - 1918) entitled, *And when did you last see your Father?* The original is in oils and hangs in the Walker Art Galleries in Liverpool, but it is reproduced in a number of art books. The painting is set in the English Civil War, and shows a small boy, dressed in Cavalier's clothes, being questioned by six sombrely dressed Parliamentarians. The tension in the room is reflected in the worried faces of the women folk, and the looks that the depicted figures are giving the boy. From the painting, one cannot tell whether the boy will tell his questioners anything, but it does imply that the whole family are facing some kind of inquisition, to establish the whereabouts of the father, and probably their political allegiance. If these suspected Royalists were confirmed as supporters of the King, then their house could have been requisitioned, and they would face real hardship.

The picture represents an incident from the period in which Parliament was born, and is therefore useful in relation to the emergence of citizenship and the birth of democratic government. Through close attention to the details in the painting, some of the pressure of the depicted situation can be recreated, and the major human theme of loyalty can be investigated. Initially, the children have the roles of aristocratic Royalists and servants in the household, later, some take up roles on the opposing side as the interrogating Parliamentarians.

The drama conventions highlighted are **hot seating** and **freeze frame**. The former is ideally suited to the interrogation elements of this drama, and is a valuable probing technique to develop knowledge of the character's motives, attitudes and values. Freeze frames are also employed fully as they can convey much more than words, and their flexibility makes them particularly useful here.

Avoiding the children's suggestions and responses in order to follow the plan may mean that real opportunities for relevant learning are missed. A professional balance between objectives and children's interests is always required.

Teaching Objectives and Learning Areas

- Consciously shape the dramatic space and place objects and roles within it (*the imagination*).
- Deliberately vary the volume, intonation and tenor of the language used (*language*).
- Distinguish between personal feelings and those of the roles portrayed (*reflection*).

Prior Experience and Materials

The children need to be aware of the basic historical context behind this story in order to appreciate the full significance of this incident. It is a useful drama to provide some historical chronology between the National Curriculum requirements of the Tudors and the Victorians.

- A good colour reproduction of the painting in a book.
- Photocopies of the painting.
- Paper and pens.

First Encounters: Creating the Drama Context

A ROYALIST HOUSEHOLD

- Carry out some preliminary research or brief information sharing about the period of the Civil War between the Puritans, or Roundheads as they were called, and the Royalists, or Cavaliers, and the political differences between them. This might include social history including the costumes and armour of the times likely to be found in the Royalist household depicted by Yeames, in contrast to a Puritan household.

- Ask the children to express their understanding of the period in an improvisation or freeze frame depicting either the servants of a Royalist household greeting the returning head of the family or a Puritan family choosing their clothes in a London shop.

- Show a colour reproduction of the picture to the class and then provide each group with a copy of the resource picture and discuss together what events might have led up to the moment depicted.

- In pairs, design and draw the crest of the Royalist family and compose their motto. Place these around the walls of the drama space and re-arrange the furniture to make a room in their house.

THE FATHER LEAVES TO JOIN THE KING

- In role as the father, the head of the household, call the class as your servants together, and explain that you are leaving to join King Charles I and his army at Oxford. Ask them to continue to serve your family as faithfully as they have over past generations and remind them they are living in dangerous and uncertain times. The Roundheads have grown stronger since the battle of Naseby, which they won. Ask them how they'll support your wife and children, especially if you never return.

- Out of role, ask the class to suggest happy memories, which the servants might have, of working for this family. Then place an empty chair representing the father in the centre of the drama space and explain that each child's distance from the chair represents the proximity in time of their memory to the present moment of his departure. Ask the children to take up a position orientated to the chair, which represents their memory. Do two or three of these, and circulate around the class asking a few individuals about the occasions they are recalling.

- Then change this to an unhappy memory about working for the family. The children need to place themselves in relationship to the chair, which now symbolises the family, according to the strength of their negative feeling towards them. So those with strong negative feelings will be far away and vice versa. Again, ask a few individuals about the occasion they're remembering.

THE ROUNDHEADS ARRIVE

- As a class create a series of sequential group freeze frames which develop the moment of the painting, e.g. groups could show:

a) The family saying goodbye to the father.

b) The family preparing themselves to meet the Parliamentarians.

c) The servants in the kitchens whilst the interrogation takes place.

d) The picture itself (this involves 14 people).

- Observe these in order and as teacher comment upon the tensions and fears you see expressed in these silent portrayals.

- Look carefully at the picture again together and generate ideas about the papers on the table. For example are they anonymous letters informing on the family, or instructions for the Roundheads' interrogation?

- As a class or in pairs, compose one of these written documents and explain how they came to be in the Roundheads' possession.

- Draw the children's attention to the large open chest in the picture and discuss what it might contain and what the father might have taken out of it.

- Suggest to the class, that the box being held by one of the Parliamentarians contains something of vital importance to the situation. In pairs, ask the class to role play two Parliamentarians placing objects and papers inside it. Allow snippets of these conversations to be shared.

- With the whole class, brainstorm possible reasons and excuses why the father is not in the house, and consider what might the Parliamentarians reactions be to these excuses.

Conflicts and Tensions: Developing the Drama

THE ROUNDHEADS USE COERCION

- In role, as one of the leading Parliamentarians, call all the children as servants of the household into the main kitchen, explaining that on the orders of Oliver Cromwell, the house is being temporarily requisitioned for the use of your officers and soldiers. State the Parliamentarian political position, and complain about the King's autocratic attitude towards the House of Commons, try to offer a balanced account of the situation the country faces. Make it clear you need to speak to the owner of the house, to ascertain whether he supports the King and request their co-operation, as reasonable people, regardless of their political views.

- Question the servants, by calling a few at a time out to face you, and ask them to give you information about the father and the family, e.g. when they last saw him what had the family been doing? Who had they been seeing recently? Try to find out individual attitudes towards the father and this family, does anyone hold a grudge against them, or disagree with their politics? Conclude this session with the announcement that all members of the family and their servants are to remain on the premises 'for their own safety'.

CAPTIVES AT HOME

- In a new role as one of the servants, discuss with the other servants, the class, your different options for action, and point out the reality of the Roundheads' overwhelming power in this situation. Consider making up excuses or reasons for people to be released from the room and the house, e.g. different requests to a guard on the door, notes to the officer in charge asking for an interview.

- Suggest a few individuals are allowed out, under escort, to meet the officer and be questioned about their request. Let a group role play this in front of the class with you as the officer.

- Suggest that one guard is bribed to carry a note to a friend in a nearby village. Ask the children to write these notes, then swap them to read each other's and listen to a few.

- In small groups, improvise conversations at the local alehouse in which rumour and gossip about what's happening in the household abound.

Resolutions: Drawing the Drama Together

THE FINAL HEARING

- Explain that you wish to return to the moment of the picture, and build a courtroom atmosphere through altering the room layout in line with the picture. Ask for volunteers to be the interrogating Parliamentarians and the members of the family and staff. Provide time for group discussion and generation of possible questions and ideas.

- Ask the child who volunteered to be the mother to come forward and set up a variation on decision alley; a thought passage down which she walks towards her interrogation, listening to her thoughts and fears which are expressed aloud. Set up two lines of children, (from the family or staff) facing each other and let her mind speak to her as she walks past. Alternatively, this could be undertaken for the little boy in the picture.

- In role as the chief interrogator, when the mother reaches the end of the passage and the scene is set, demand she come before you and your fellow Parliamentarians to be questioned. For example, you might ask about who she has visited recently, does she know any Royalists, what does she think of Cromwell, you note there is little money in the house to whom has she given it, what's her religion and so on. Draw in other members of the family and staff and interrogate the children in role, inviting your fellow Parliamentarians to ask questions as well. Use the contents of the box in the improvisation, and perhaps order a soldier to examine the contents of the open chest, and question the family about that too.

- Conclude with small group freeze frames that portray the conclusion of this episode. Ask groups to title these and include the servants in their image. Observe all of these together.

- Discuss with the children, their perceptions of the issues, particularly relating to loyalty and moral duty and the tensions which these created in this context. Also consider what individuals felt and did whilst making the drama, help them to identify the changing pressures and their feelings, and consider the interplay between being in role, being yourself, and being a member of a group.

Extension Activities

- The final scene could be rewritten as a play script, indicating the characters' moves and words, as well as the props, costumes, scenery and character resumés. This makes good use of both the painting and the drama.

- The image of the Royalists & Cavaliers through history has been romantic and flamboyantly attractive, in comparison to the dour image of the Roundheads & Parliamentarians, yet the values which underpin our present political system, are nearer to the latter. The relationship of the image/medium to the message can be discussed, and contemporary examples examined that show how individuals, pressure groups and governments seek to project themselves.

- Discuss how children and victims should be questioned or treated in court, and the issue of what credibility can be attached to their witness, when they are in situations of great duress.

Resourcing Further Drama from Pictures

A variety of visual art can be used to resource drama; reproductions of oil paintings or sketches, photographs, sculpture, objects, photo stories and illustrations from picture books. Those that imply a narrative and show tense and dramatic incidents are perhaps easiest to use, as are those that show detailed portrayals of characters or a strong evocation of atmosphere and environment. In offering a clear sense of the people, place or predicament, visual art begins to resource the narrative that the class seeks to examine. Pictures are particularly helpful for developing historical drama, although research and reading about the period are also needed to enhance the drama.

Combining pictures with poetry, proverbs or a paragraph from a text is another powerful drama resource, since both verbal and non-verbal modes offer the class material, which they can connect to and elaborate upon. An extremely useful text for such work is *Paintings with Words* by Michael and Peter Benton (1995, Hodder and Stoughton). This is an inspired collection of paired paintings and poems, many of which involve writers responding to a particular painting by making a poem about it, or vice versa. Good examples are John Keat's poem *La Belle Dame Sans Merci* with Frank Dicksee and John Waterhouse's paintings inspired by the verse, as well as Pieter Brueghel's '*The Return of the Hunters*' and John Berryman and Anne Stevenson's poems inspired by his painting. If picture book images are used, and many are powerfully illustrated, it is preferable that the children do not know the story within them.

In using pictures, the visual should be shown to the class to arouse interest and in small groups, ideas and questions generated about the people, place or predicament portrayed. For example, who are the people shown, what are they doing, and what's their relationship to one another? In using their ideas, the groups might bring the picture to life through an improvisation or depict it as a freeze frame suggesting aloud what individuals are thinking. The predicament may be shown more clearly through flashbacks, flash-forwards and conventions that examine context and character, and a drama is built around the situation. Some painters, like Lowry and Brueghel for example, evoke a clear sense of place, so the class could list the people living or visiting the place shown and the problems they might encounter. In voting to agree the narrative elements, a drama can be built upon their ideas. We recommend the following:

PAINTINGS

The Dutch School (1666) *The Fire of London*, Museum of London.
John Everett Millais (1852) *Ophelia*, The Tate Gallery, London.
Vincent Van Gogh (1890) *Prisoners Exercising*, Pushkin Museum, Moscow.
Henri Rousseau (1897) *The Sleeping Gypsy*, Museum of Modern Art, New York.
Andrew Wyeth (1948) *Christina's World*, Museum of Modern Art, New York.
Edward Hopper (1949) *Conference at Night*, Wichita Art Museum, Kansas.

ILLUSTRATIONS FROM PICTURE BOOKS

Antonia Barber, illus. P.J. Lynch (1996) *Catkin*, Walker.
Marilee Heyer (1988) *The Weaving of a Dream,* Puffin.
Richard Keens Douglas (1995) *Freedom Child of the Sea*, Annick.
Geraldine McCaughrean, illus. Gary Blythe (1999) *Beauty and the Beast*, Doubleday.
Paul Owen Lewis (1995) *Storm Boy*, Barefoot.
Jane Yolen, illus. David Shannon (1992) *Encounter*, Harcourt Brace Jovanovich.

Chapter 10
A POEM: THE HIGHWAYMAN
BY ALFRED NOYES

THE HIGHWAYMAN
Alfred Noyes
illustrated by CHARLES KEEPING
OXFORD

Introduction

This drama is based upon the narrative poem *The Highwayman*, by Alfred Noyes, which is powerfully illustrated by Charles Keeping in the 1981 Oxford edition which won the Kate Greenaway Medal. The poem is read at intervals during the drama to provide a context for dramatic investigation and to guide the examination.

The poem is a melodramatic, love-story between a Highwayman and Bess, a landlord's daughter, it is set in the eighteenth century. Their relationship arouses the jealousy of Tim, the ostler, (a stablehand) who, the reader supposes, tips off King George's soldiers on the whereabouts of the Highwayman, and his likely return to the girl. The soldiers lay a trap, gagging Bess and tying her up to her bed, but leaving a loaded musket beside her, with the muzzle resting beneath her breast. She twists and turns and eventually fires the gun, to warn the Highwayman of the danger as he approaches, but of course in doing so she kills herself. Later, when the Highwayman hears of the cost of his escape, he is so enraged, that he gallops back to the inn to wreak his revenge, only to be gunned down on the highroad by the waiting soldiers. The poem concludes with the image of the lovers' ghostly reunion at the inn.

In this drama, the conventions, **role on the wall** and **mime** are highlighted. The former is used in order to heighten the children's understanding of the motivation and feelings of the characters. Outlines of the Highwayman and Bess are created and emotional perspectives are added to this role on the wall, which combines reflection and expression in a strong visual form. Mime is used to explore a premonition of impending disaster and therefore to 'control' the evidence which might be shown.

Avoiding the children's suggestions and responses in order to follow the plan may mean that real opportunities for relevant learning are missed. A professional balance between the teaching objectives and children's interests is always required.

Teaching Objectives and Learning Areas

- Develop and maintain different roles and perspectives (*the imagination*).
- Tolerate uncertainty and ambiguity in the drama (*personal and social skills*).
- Manipulate conventions with imagination and some degree of independence (*the drama process*).

Prior Experience and Materials

The children may have some knowledge of the social and economic conditions of the period, but this is not necessary. It is preferable if the poem has not been read or studied before.

- A copy of *The Highwayman* by A. Noyes, illustrated C. Keeping, Oxford.
- Large pieces of paper, pens.
- Photocopies of the illustration of Bess bound and gagged.
- Photocopies of the concluding pictures of the ghosts

First Encounters: Creating the Drama Context

THE ROADS, INNS AND HIGHWAYMEN OF THE EIGHTEENTH CENTURY

- Give the children the title of the poem that is to be the basis of the drama and briefly contextualise and introduce the period through discussion of the social and economic conditions. Make the point that policing was carried out by the King's army. Discuss how people travelled around the country, and the prevalence and notoriety of highwaymen in this era.
- Ask the children to create group freeze frames that represent their understanding of one scene in everyday life, as it would have been at the time of the poem.
- Tell the class the drama is going to be about a Highwayman, an innkeeper and his daughter Bess, a stableman/ostler Tim, and some soldiers. Then read up to the arrival of King George's soldiers and the lines *'they said no word to the landlord. They drank his ale instead'*. Show the pictures throughout, as these offer evidence of the period, and are striking and powerful.

TWO VIOLENT DEATHS

- Explain you want to start the drama at this point, and take up the role, tone and manner of a newspaper editor, alerting your journalists, the class, to a rumour about a sensational story: the violent death of two people, a man and a woman. Only sketch the merest details, it will be the children's task as reporters to investigate these, but refer to the involvement of the authorities, and tell them that the deaths took place at a notorious Public House on the Toll-Pike road. Tell the children that the girl's body had been found upstairs in a bedroom, and the man's outside on the road. Mention that there were rumours of hostages and informers being involved and suggest they go to the scene to uncover the truth.
- Out of role, ask a boy and a girl to lie down upon separate pieces of paper, as though they were the bodies of Bess, and the Highwayman. Ask two other children to draw around these 'bodies', and write their fictional names on the top of the paper. Then pin them onto the wall of the drama space. These are the empty roles on the wall, into which the children will write their thoughts and feelings, at points decided by you.

- Divide the children into small groups and ask them to identify the kind of person they might want to interview, to write the story, and then to brainstorm the questions they'd need to ask as journalists. Those people may well not appear in the actual poem, but list them on the board and prioritise them, e.g. Tim, the soldiers and their captain, the inn keeper and his wife, Bess's sister, a traveller, locals in the inn and so on. In doing this you will identify both the issues and the people with whom your drama can engage.

- Ask each child to write the one question they most want answered on the space outside one of the roles on the wall.

> Who was there at the time they were killed?
> How many times was the gun shot or the rope tied around the dead girl?
> What were they doing when they were shot?
> Did they know each other?
> Why was one tied?
> Why was Dick's horse shot?
> Why did the soldiers shoot them?
> What evidence do the soldiers have that they needed to die?
> Did Bess or Dick do anything to upset the King or the soldiers, so they would kill them?

(11-12 Year Olds)

INVESTIGATING THE WITNESSES

- In pairs, ask the children to briefly prepare questions to put to two agreed individuals.

- In role, as one of the chosen interviewees, allow yourself to be hot seated about your knowledge, actions and movements last night.

- Invite volunteers or select children to take up the role of another interviewee and be questioned. The poem implies the informer was Tim, but a number of people could have told the authorities about the Highwayman's return.

- In role as the newspaper editor, ask your journalists what has been revealed and who else might fruitfully be questioned. For instance, the soldiers behaved in a very intimidating fashion, what were their orders?

- At some point the children will become impatient for the investigation to move forward following the narrative, you'll have to judge this, and then read more of the poem, up to the point where the girl warns her lover with her own death and the Highwayman gallops off.

The father seemed sad that he had to bury his daughter. He didn't have many answers.

Was Bess killed in room 4 or in another room and then bought to the room 4. If so what would be the point?

The soldiers were very fidgety. They look like they knew everything about the killing. Bess's father looked scared, as if he was going to be killed too.

I know Bess's father is upset but how did he know that four soldiers killed his daughter? He must have a connection with the murder. I need to talk to the general.

Were the soldiers really soldiers? They didn't seem like it.

(11-12 Year Olds)

Conflicts and Tensions: Developing the Drama

THE INFORMER AND THE SOLDIERS

- Discuss with the children the likelihood of Tim, the ostler, being the informer, since he is in love with Bess and jealous of the Highwayman. Suggest that he might not have been able to face the Captain of the soldiers himself, so he could have written a note of betrayal. Ask the children individually to write this note and then exchange these with someone else. Share a few of these.

- In role as the captain, call the class, as your company of soldiers together, and demand they apprehend the Highwayman. Brief them on this risky job, the man is an armed and ruthless criminal. Authorise using the girl Bess, as bait for the trap, but do not specify how they are to treat her. Conclude this briefing with the caution that if it is to be successful their work must have the utmost secrecy attached to it. As a consequence, the soldiers are, not allowed to leave barracks, all personal arrangements must be cancelled. No information about the assignment can be shared.

- In pairs, ask the children to role-play the conversation between one of the soldiers, and his friend/wife/girlfriend, who arrive to 'go out on the town' that evening. They must put them off with excuses, in order to maintain the secrecy of the forthcoming operation. Discuss whether suspicions may have been aroused.

THE LOVERS

- In small groups, devise and mime a premonition that Bess or the Highwayman dreamt, before the incidents in the poem.

- In threes, role play Bess's parents talking to her about her interest in or relationship with the Highwayman and their fears for her. Listen to snatches of these.

- Place the roles on the walls on the floor and ask the children to either write inside Bess's outline her thoughts and views, or write in her parents' thoughts about her or the Highwayman outside the appropriate outline.

- Invite two children to be hot seated as the couple. Provide time for the class to think of questions to put to them about their expectations for the future.

Resolutions: Drawing the Drama Together

THE FIRST SHOT

- Use the drama space to represent the main public bar of the Inn, and agree the position of the bar-counter and fireplace. Discuss who might have been at the Inn and their relationship to the lovers, if they had one. As a whole class improvise the scene in the bar immediately before the shot. Everyone knows most of the soldiers are in the room above them. Freeze the action and re-read the extract from the poem, from '*But he gagged his daughter*' to '*and warned him, with her death.*'

- Circulate around the Inn and ask individuals to speak out loud their thoughts at the moment the shot rang out.

- The death of the girl is both a surprise and a mistake for the soldiers. Give out copies of the picture of Bess gagged and ask small groups to discuss the soldiers' response to the situation. Some may not have liked the way she was treated, what will they say to the Captain and her parents?

- In role as the Captain, gather your soldiers together and demand to know why and how she died. Conclude the discussion with considering how you can still arrest the wretched Highwayman.

- Read the rest of the poem to the class, showing the illustrations as you do so.

- Give out copies of the last visuals of the lovers as ghosts. Place two chairs in the drama space, and ask two children to sit on them, as Bess and the Highwayman, with their backs to the class. Invite the children to come out and place their hand on a character's shoulder and speak out loud the thoughts of one of the ghosts. Begin this slowly and with concentration.
- Let the class write these thoughts into the inside of the roles on the wall of Bess and the Highwayman.
- Read out the inner and outer writing on the roles on the wall, including the questions originally asked.
- Discuss with the class their feelings about the narrative and whether their questions were answered. What questions and puzzles still remain?

Extension Activities

- Writing possibilities include the journalists' news reports, the dossier of crimes which the Highwayman was alleged to have committed, the Captain's report of the incidents, and the bereaved parents' letters to relatives about their daughter's death.
- The consequences for Tim, the ostler, could be investigated and portrayed, in order to provide a further dimension to his character.
- Alternative endings could be constructed and portrayed through drama. These could be retold years later.
- The girl's sacrifice, the ostler's betrayal and the behaviour of the authorities, has parallels in other times, connections could be identified and discussed.

Resourcing Further Drama from Poetry

Since much poetry investigates issues and reflects upon experience, it is a valuable resource for drama. Poetry offers children layers of potential meanings to explore, and although in classroom drama, the text itself is not literally enacted, dramatic exploration can create a deeper reading of the poem. Multiple interpretations and perspectives can be examined in action, and verses can be read aloud during the drama to create atmosphere. Later, the poem can be visited for a closer linguistic examination, when the range of insights evoked can be discussed in relation to the evidence in the text. Narrative verse is particularly useful, since it can provide a compete tale to guide the drama. Selected verses of the chosen poem can also be used, or just the title and a dramatic exploration built around this. Poems, illustrated as picture books are rich resources for drama, as the illustrations too evoke meanings. Poems we recommend include the following:

Maya Angelou *Life Doesn't Frighten Me at All* (1993) Illus: J M Basquiat, Stewart, Tabori, Chang.
Robert Browning *The Pied Piper of Hamelin* (1993) Illus: André Amstutz, Orchard.
Charles Causley 'On St Catherine's Day', 'Bramblepark', 'Francesco de la Vega', 'Maggie Dooley' in *Jack the Treacle Eater* (1987) Illus: Charles Keeping, MacMillan.
Roy Gerrard *Sir Francis Drake; his Daring Deeds* (1988) Victor Gollancz
Roy Gerrard *Rosie and the Rustlers* (1989) Victor Gollancz.
Henry Longfellow *Hiawatha* (1996) Illus: Susan Jeffers, Puffin.
Percy Bysse Shelley (2000) Illus: Theo Gayer-Anderson, Hoopoe
Clark Taylor *The House that Crack Built* (1992) Illus: Jan Thomson Dicks, Chronicle.
Alfred Lord Tennyson *The Lady of Shalott* (1986) Illus: Charles Keeping, Oxford.
Robert Frost '*Stopping by Woods on a Snowy Evening*', Felicicia Hemans '*Casablanca*', Walter de la Mare '*The Listeners*', in The Oxford Treasury of Classic Poems (1996) eds: Michael Harrison and Christopher Clark, Oxford

Chapter 11

A DIARY: ANNE FRANK: THE DIARY OF A YOUNG GIRL

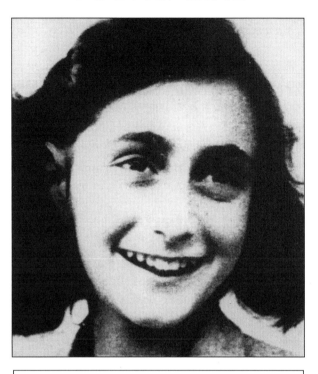

'I want to go on living after my death. And therefore I am grateful to God for giving me this gift of expressing all that is in me'

Introduction

This diary was written by Anne Frank, a thirteen year old Jewess who, with her family and some friends, went into hiding from the Gestapo in Amsterdam between 1942-1944. It is an extraordinary account of their day-to-day living in this refuge and has become a widely known and celebrated text. It retains an enormous freshness and poignancy, although it was never finished because of Anne's arrest and death in the concentration camp at Belsen, only a few short months before the liberation. The diary is read aloud to a particular entry and provides the context in which the drama develops. Later entries from the diary are also read aloud during the drama for information about events and Anne's perspective upon them.

There are several versions of the diaries, all of them authentic, which you could use. The most recent volume, with an introduction and commentary by Otto Frank, her father, is *The Definitive Edition: The Diary of a Young Girl*, (1997) Penguin. The drama examines the persecution of the Jews in Nazi Germany seen through the eyes of Anne, who, towards the close of the drama goes into hiding in the secret flat in her father's spice factory. Despite her plight and relative imprisonment however, Anne did continue to hear about the lives of those in the city who were living in dreadful conditions of fear. The fugitives had constant access to the outside world through intermediaries, but could never venture out into the street for fear of discovery.

The drama conventions focused upon in this drama are **whole group improvisation** and **writing in role**. The former, often led by the teacher involves creating a situation together through improvisation. The rough shape of this may have been discussed beforehand, but relevant and unexpected developments will still emerge. Writing in role is used to provoke thinking in role in order to capture a factory worker's perspective in first person narrative, as a parallel to Anne's own narrative in her diary.

Avoiding the children's suggestions and responses in order to follow the plan may mean that real opportunities for relevant learning are missed. A professional balance between teaching objectives and children's interests is always required.

Teaching Objectives and Learning Areas

* Consider with increasing depth the moral issues of persecution and prejudice in the drama (*personal and social skills*).
* Integrate factual knowledge into the drama (*the content of the drama*).
* Recognise common threads and similarities in the drama and the real world (*reflection*).

Prior Experience and Materials

This could usefully be set within a study of the Second World War and the events which led up to it. Some knowledge about the rise of the Nazis and The Final Solution is essential. The early entries of the diary, up to 5th July 1942 need to have been read to the class.
* A copy of *Anne Frank: The Diary of a Young Girl*.
* Large poster size pieces of paper and felt-tip pens.
* Photocopies of the diary entry Wed. 8th July 1942.

First Encounters: Creating the Drama Context

THE SPICE FACTORY
* Remind the class of what you've read in Anne's diary, up to the end of 5 July 1942, and of her father's position as the general manager of a spice processing and packing factory in Amsterdam.
* In small groups, set the task of designing, drawing and composing an advertising poster for one of the spices that might have been prepared in the factory, paying particular attention to the faraway and exotic nature of its country of origin. The poster might also contain a recipe for some 'foreign' food, which uses the spice. These posters should be large enough to be displayed in the classroom/drama space.
* Ask the children to decide upon a role they will adopt as a worker in the factory, and suggest they make a freeze-frame of a group at work in the factory. All the groups should do this together. Count to three and suggest the factory comes to life, with you in role too joining in the day's work for a few minutes.
* In the same groups, ask the children to draw a plan of the factory, which includes a secret annexe in which people could hide in times of emergency.
* Ask each person to think of an item (e.g. a wireless) that might be put in the secret annexe, and explain to a someone why they chose it.
* In their groups, ask them to work out a system of communication between the main factory and the occupants of the secret annexe. This may be used for warnings, but also for other messages so the occupants know a friend is communicating.

THE FIRST OFFICIAL VISIT

- Whilst this is being planned, go into role as a Nazi official visiting the factory, and begin an inspection with the Heil Hitler salute. Your manner should be clipped and severe, stride around the room and question individuals about who they are and where they come from. This portrayal of Nazi power needs to be carefully effected, being just on the edge of open aggression, with the manner of a bully still using coercion rather than physical force. At some point in your visit notice the posters, and begin to make racist comments about them: the place of origin, the types of food and the people who eat such food. You *might* deface some by scrawling a Star of David on them, or even rip some down and destroy them. Culminate your visit by making threats against the factory and announce that interviews will take place shortly to establish the racial purity of the workers. In order to prove their correctness; they will need to give information about any foreigners they know and others who are different. Then leave.

- In role as one of the factory workers, call everyone together for the midday break, and discuss how to prepare for the return visit of the official. Try to play as small a part in this as possible, perhaps only reminding those children who suggest using violence, that this response was not a realistic one. You could mention the Warsaw Ghetto uprising, which, whilst it was relatively near the end of the war, resulted in the crushing of the uprising and the death of the resistance fighters.

- Ask the children to list the attributes which make them similar to other pupils, and list all the things that make them different.

- Discuss the two lists in general with the class, deciding which items are significant and why.

- Conclude this episode by writing the diary entry of one of the workers at the factory that day. Mention they will be making further diary entries in this role later in the drama.

Conflicts and Tensions: Developing the Drama

THE SECOND VISIT AND THE INTERROGATION

- Ask the class to make one large freeze frame of the factory at work five minutes before the return of the official, and bring this to life briefly.

- Interrupt this by narrating the arrival of the official and soldiers who surround the factory to prevent anyone from leaving. In role as the official, make everyone sit in silence on the floor, spaced out in lines. If there are incidents, which disturb these orders, ask the children to portray the arrest of those involved. These should be freeze-framed in groups and composed very quickly, to make the point that physical resistance is futile.

- In role as the official, sort the children into two or three large groups, according to some personal physical criteria, such as size, hair colour or eye colour, but do not tell them how or why you are doing this.

- Set up a table and two chairs facing each other, possibly with a tape recorder. Then in role as the official, arbitrarily call children out to be questioned about both the factory and their fellow workers. Write down occasional details and begin to focus upon minority groups. Questions should also begin to probe how the factory is run, how it is laid out and the possibility of hiding places. The initial interviewing should involve three or four children at most, enough for everyone to feel the measure of the occasion.

- Each of the interviewees will need to be questioned in a manner appropriate to them as individuals, their personality and experience of drama. Use your personal professional knowledge of the children; the degree of stress put upon each child should be well within each child's tolerance.

- Out of role, discuss with the class what they have seen and heard, the motives of the official, and how interviewees would be advised to behave.

- Ask the children to complete another diary entry in role as a factory worker about the segregation of the workers and the interrogation. Share some extracts of these and provide an opportunity to express lingering questions and discuss any negative feelings. Explain to the class that Nazi prejudice was not simply anti-Semitic, and discuss these issues.

Wednesday, 8th July, 1942

Dear Kitty,

Years seemed to have passed between Sunday and now. So much has happened, it is just as if the whole world had turned upside down. But I am still alive, Kitty, and that is the main thing, Daddy says.

Yes, I'm still alive, indeed, but don't ask where or how. You wouldn't understand a word, so I will begin by telling you what happened on Sunday afternoon.

At three o'clock (Harry had just gone, but was coming back later) someone rang the front door bell. I was lying lazily reading a book on the veranda in the sunshine, so didn't hear it. A bit later, Margot appeared at the kitchen door looking very excited. "The S.S. have sent a call-up notice for Daddy," she whispered. "Mummy has gone to see Mr. Van Daan already." (Van Daan is a friend who works with Daddy in the business.) It was a great shock to me, a call-up; everyone knows what that means. I picture concentration camps and lonely cells—should we allow him to be doomed to this? "Of course he won't go," declared Margot, while we waited together. "Mummy has gone to the Van Daans to discuss whether we should move into our hiding-place tomorrow. The Van Daans are going with us, so we shall be seven in all." Silence. We couldn't talk any more, thinking about Daddy, who, little knowing what was going on, was visiting some old people in the Joodse Invalide*; waiting for Mummy, the heat and suspense, all made us very overawed and silent.

Suddenly the bell rang again. "That is Harry," I said. "Don't open the door." Margot held me back, but it was not necessary as we heard Mummy and Mr. Van Daan downstairs, talking to Harry, then they came in and closed the door behind them. Each time the bell went, Margot or I had to creep softly down to see if it was Daddy, not opening the door to anyone else.

Margot and I were sent out of the room. Van Daan wanted to talk to Mummy alone. When we were alone together in our bedroom, Margot told me that the call-up was not for Daddy, but for her. I was more frightened than ever and began to cry. Margot is sixteen; would they really take girls of that age away alone? But thank goodness she won't go. Mummy said so herself; that must be what Daddy meant when he talked about us going into hiding.

Into hiding—where would we go, in a town or the country, in a house or a cottage, when, how, where . . . ?

These were questions I was not allowed to ask, but I couldn't get them out of my mind. Margot and I began to pack some of our most vital belongings into a school satchel. The first thing I put in was this diary, then hair-curlers, handkerchiefs, school books, a comb, old letters; I put in the craziest things with the idea that we were going into hiding. But I'm not sorry, memories mean more to me than dresses.

At five o'clock Daddy finally arrived, and we rang up Mr. Koophuis to ask if he could come round in the evening. Van Daan went and fetched Miep. Miep has been in the business with Daddy since 1933 and has become a close

* Jewish Charitable Institution.

friend, likewise her brand-new husband, Henk. Miep came and took some shoes, dresses, coats, underwear, and stockings away in her bag, promising to return in the evening. Then silence fell on the house; not one of us felt like eating anything, it was still hot and everything was very strange. We let our large upstairs room to a certain Mr. Goudsmit, a divorced man in the thirties, who appeared to have nothing to do on this particular evening; we simply could not get rid of him without being rude; he hung about until ten o'clock. At eleven o'clock Miep and Henk Van Santen arrived. Once again, shoes, stockings, books, and underclothes disappeared into Miep's bag and Henk's deep pockets, and at eleven-thirty they too disappeared. I was dog-tired, and although I knew that it would be my last night in my own bed I fell asleep immediately and didn't wake up until Mummy called me at 5.30 the next morning. Luckily it was not so hot as Sunday; warm rain fell steadily all day. We put on heaps of clothes as if we were going to the North Pole, the sole reason being to take clothes with us. No Jew in our situation would have dreamt of going out with a suitcase full of clothing. I had on two vests, three pairs of knickers, a dress, on top of that a skirt, jacket, summer coat, two pairs of stockings, lace-up shoes, woolly cap, scarf and still more; I was nearly stifled before we started, but no one inquired about that.

Margot filled her satchel with school books, fetched her bicycle and rode off behind Miep into the unknown, as far as I was concerned. You see I still didn't know where our secret hiding-place was to be. At seven thirty the door closed behind us. Moortie, my little cat, was the only creature to whom I said farewell. She would have a good home with the neighbours. This was all written in a letter addressed to Mr. Goudsmit.

There was one pound of meat in the kitchen for the cat, breakfast things lying on the table, stripped beds, all giving the impression that we had left helter-skelter. But we didn't care about impressions, we only wanted to get away, only escape and arrive safely, nothing else. Continued tomorrow.

Yours, ANNE.

FATE AND FLIGHT

- Split the class into small groups to discuss what the workers' families might do to ensure their safety.

- Tell the children that probably many Jewish families from the factory, chose to leave their homes at short notice. The only possessions that they could take were ones they could carry or wear without raising the suspicions of the Nazis or the collaborating police. Ask them to list the things they would take with them and what they would hide about their bodies and or pack into bags.

- Hand out copies of Anne's diary entry for Wednesday 8 July 1942, this describes the Frank family's flight. Let the children read this individually.

- Conclude this section of the narrative with group freeze frames, of families' responses at the time, e.g. being arrested, arriving at a concentration camp, entering the safety of an annexe, or boarding a train for some distant destination. Observe these together and ask children from other groups to offer the thoughts and words of the family members shown.

- Read Anne's diary entries for 9, 10 and 11 July 1942 to the class. Discuss the situation.

THE FRANK FAMILY IN HIDING: THE ROWS

- The drama now shifts to focusing more upon Anne and her family. The explorations suggested relate to themes in her diary including discord, fear and anger and are tied to particular diary entries. It is possible to read the full text over time, stopping at the places mentioned to open up some drama or just to select a few to explore in a single session.

- Read the first paragraph of the entry on Sunday, 27 September 1942, which describes a row Anne had with her mother.

- Improvise the row in pairs (or threes, including Margot her sister), following a brief discussion about the likely themes of the row and the pressures of being cooped up in the secret annexe. Observe a few.

- In forum theatre, role play Anne's parents and the Van Daan's discussing the three children that night, this also turned into a quarrel. Invite four children to take up the roles of the parents, and prepare their improvisation whilst the rest of the class discuss Anne's attitude to the adults. Both the actors and the observers have the right to halt the action in the forum, if they feel the actors need help or the scene is losing authenticity. Individuals or groups then offer advice to different characters and suggest alternative words and actions, which adjust the tone. The drama is then revisited using the ideas put forward.

- Suggest that Anne overheard the adults' row from her bedroom, and ask the class to write her diary entry for that night.

- Read Anne's own account of these two rows on Sunday 27 and Monday 28 September 1942.

THE FRANK FAMILY IN HIDING: THE FEAR AND THE BURGLARY

- Read Anne's diary for 10, 12, 17 and 19 November 1942 which describe Albert Dussel coming to live with the family in the annexe, and the news he brings of the persecution of the Jews. Ask groups to create a sound and action collage that represents Anne's half-formed nightmare that night. Ritual chanting or words and phrases could be added to reflect Anne's growing fears and concerns. Share these together.

- Read the diary entry for Saturday 27 November 1943 when Anne, almost asleep sees an image of Lies, her Jewish friend, calling for help to *rescue me from this hell*. Discuss with the class what might be happening to Lies, and show group freeze-frames of her, wherever she is now. Title these and observe them.

- Read the entry for Wednesday 29 December, a month later when Anne again worries for Lies, and compares her own existence in the secret hideout with her friend's probable existence.

- Read Tuesday 11 April 1944 to the words, *'what happened? Tell us quickly!'* This entry describes the burglary downstairs and the impending arrival of the police. Ask pairs to create the urgent whispers of Mr and Mrs Frank as they climbed the stairs quickly into the attic.

- In role as Mr Van Daan, interrupt the whispers by exclaiming *'The police!'* and prompt a whole class mime taking up positions of fear in the attic. Let silence reign for a few moments. Then circulate slowly around the class asking children to offer their thoughts.

Resolutions: Drawing the Drama Together

'I WANT TO GO ON LIVING AFTER MY DEATH'

- Read the epilogue and discuss the persecution of the Jews, Anne's death and the diary as a written testament of her life.

- Ask groups to create a piece of sculpture, to reflect one of the themes in Anne's life. Suggest they agree the material it is made from and a title for it. Observe each one together, and discuss where such a sculpture might be placed in memory of Anne.

- Ask each child to write a paragraph to appear under the piece of sculpture in the museum/park/other venue decided upon.

Extension Activities

- The themes reflected in the sculptures can be discussed in relation to parallel conflicts around the world. The class could display the titles in their sculptures and make posters of these with newspaper cuttings to show the contemporary relevance of Anne's persecution and prejudice.

- The plight of other children in World War II could be examined through drama and literature circles, supported by texts such as Michelle Magorian's *Goodnight Mr Tom*, (Puffin), Roberto Innocenti's *Rose Blanche*, (Jonathan Cape),or Christa Laird's *But Can the Phoenix Sing?* (Julia MacRae).

- The arrival of the allied liberators to investigate the persecution and the Nuremburg trials themselves, offer opportunities to examine the Nazis record over the whole period.

Resourcing Further Drama from Diaries

Diaries, letters, reports and other kinds of first hand accounts are often very powerful resources for drama as they have a strong sense of the author and offer insight into their emotions and perspectives as well as particular events. Primary historical evidence, e.g. Scott's diary, Samuel Pepys' diary, or Captain Cook's log all have authenticity and the power to provide access into the minds of significant historical figures. Lewis and Clarke's reports of their epic journey across America can also be used to initiate and develop drama. Autobiographical writing from more contemporary public figures is also possible to use, as is fiction written in a diary format. We recommend:

Chris Van Allsburg (1991) *The Wretched Stone*, Mifflin
Jacqueline Wilson (1991) *The Story of Tracy Beaker*, Puffin
Rachel Anderson (1996) *Letters from Heaven*, Mammoth
Sara Fanelli (2000) *Dear Diary*, Walker
Robin Klein (1985) *Penny Pollard's Diary*, Oxford
Michael Morpurgo (1995) *The Wreck of the Zanzibar*, Mammoth
William Mayne (1999) *Midnight Fayre*

Chapter: 12

A PLAY-SCRIPT: MACBETH, THE LAST DAYS OF A QUEEN BY WILLIAM SHAKESPEARE.

MACBETH

DRAMATIS PERSONÆ

DUNCAN, *King of Scotland.*

MALCOLM,
DONALBAIN, } *his sons .*

MACBETH,
BANQUO, } *Generals of the King's army.*

MACDUFF,
LENNOX,
ROSS,
MENTEITH, } *Noblemen of Scotland .*
ANGUS,
CAITHNESS,

FLEANCE, *son to Banquo.*

SIWARD, *Earl of Northumberland, General of the English forces.*

YOUNG SIWARD, *his son.*

SEYTON, *an officer attending on Macbeth.*

BOY, *son to Macduff.*

A Sergeant.
A Porter.
An Old Man.
An English Doctor.
A Scots Doctor.

LADY MACBETH.
LADY MACDUFF
Gentlewoman *attending on Lady Macbeth.*

THE WEIRD SISTERS.
HECATE.
The Ghost of Banquo.
Apparitions.

Lords, Gentlemen, Officers, Soldiers, Murderers, Attendants, AND Messengers.

THE SCENE: *Scotland and England.*

Introduction

Shakespeare's tragedy *Macbeth* is a classic, and its themes of ambition and politics, loyalty and betrayal and innocence and guilt are contemporary concerns, making it powerful material for drama.

Shakespeare's story tells how Macbeth, a loyal general of the King, on leaving the scene of a battle, has an chance meeting with some witches upon the moor, who foretell that he will become King of Scotland. This acts as a trigger to his ambition and abetted by his wife, Lady Macbeth, he murders the King confirming their predictions, and becoming King himself. However, his guilty conscience and some of the other premonitions made by the witches generate paranoid fears about the noblemen around him, and this leads to further murder. Finally the nobility can stomach him no longer, and they join forces with the sons of the murdered men, to rebel against him, marching upon him at his Castle of Dunsinane. He is killed in the battle, shortly after he has learned of Lady Macbeth's death. The circumstances of her death are not clearly elaborated and this missing information helps to give the drama its direction.

The play centres around public life and public figures, about whose private lives little is known, except when public matters, such as the murder of the King are discussed privately. The drama described here seeks to construct a biography for Lady Macbeth, and in doing so, looks carefully at her speeches in the play. It also endeavours to make a private life for her through suggesting that she had relatives, even children who are used to develop a deeper understanding of her later behaviour.

The conventions highlighted in this drama are **hot seating**, and **whole class and group role-play**. In the former, children or their teacher, assume the role of an individual in the drama to be questioned by the rest of the class. In the latter, interaction and collaboration are used to deepen understanding and to create appropriate details about possible threads in Lady Macbeth's biography, not recorded in the play.

Avoiding the children's suggestions and responses in order to follow the plan may mean that real opportunities for relevant learning are missed. A professional balance between teaching objectives and children's interests is always required.

Teaching Objectives and Learning Areas
- Develop an enhanced understanding of particular speeches (*language*).
- Maintain and critically discuss the roles and situations (*the drama process*).
- Articulate their views of each other's contributions in the drama (*reflection*).

Prior Experience and Materials
Since the drama takes place after the events of the play, the children will need to have experienced the whole narrative through reading and/or seeing versions of it. The more familiar they are with the plot and characters the richer will be their interaction.
- A chair for Malcolm's throne.
- Writing materials for each group.
- Copies of the play.
- Copies of the paraphrases of Lady Macbeth's significant speeches.

First Encounters: Creating the Drama Context
THE COURTIERS OF SCOTLAND SWEAR ALLEGIANCE
- Explain to the class that the drama is going to build on Shakespeare's play *Macbeth* and seek to construct a past for Lady Macbeth, exploring her character, speech and behaviour in order to understand her role in the play further.
- Ask the children in small groups to create freeze-frames, which express the nature of some of the characters, such as: Macbeth, Lady Macbeth, Macduff, Lady Macduff, Banquo, Malcolm, Lennox, Ross and Siward. These will be chosen by you according to how well you consider the class knows the play, they are then shown to the rest of the class, to stimulate discussion and reflection upon the play.
- With the whole class create a freeze-frame of the courtiers, priests and nobleman, at the moment when Malcolm, Duncan's son, the recent victor in battle against Macbeth, sits upon his throne for the first time. Put the throne in a prominent position with one confident and able child, representing Malcolm, about to take his seat upon it.
- Ask them whilst they are still within the whole class freeze frame, to think of the oath of allegiance they would swear to this new King of Scotland. Then, in role yourself as the Lord High Sheriff, invite them to ceremonially come up to the King, who can take his seat and kneel one by one to swear their oath. Begin this ceremony by swearing your own oath of allegiance first. If the class find this difficult, help them with possibilities, allow time for discussion to generate ideas and begin the ceremony again.

PARAPHRASES OF SOME OF LADY MACBETH'S SPEECHES

Act 1 Scene 5 lines: 34-51; Lady Macbeth.

The raven who foretells Duncan's death is hoarse from crowing on our battlements. Let my female feelings of kindness go, so that I am full of aggression, blocking my instinctive conscience, which would prevent me from doing what I want. My natural kindness must turn to disregard and hostility. My determination must not be stopped by my conscience, which needs to be ignored and forgotten by thoughts of the profits of my actions.

Act 1 Scene 5 lines: 57-67; Lady Macbeth.

King Duncan will not leave here as he wishes. Macbeth, the expression on your face tells everyone you are upset. Pretend to be happy and calm, keep your stress to yourself, and this will let what has to be done tonight be done, and bring us the power and sovereignty over the country.

Act 5 Scene 1 lines: 30-66; Lady Macbeth.

There's blood and guilt on my hands.

Go, go conscience. Its time I did it. But hell is a dreadful place. Surely you, a soldier are not afraid, why be afraid when we know that there is no one who has the power to make us afraid. I am surprised that what we did to the King has aroused so much guilt.

Macduff's wife, what of her? Can't we bury these thoughts.

Nothing will take these feelings from me.

I must pull myself together and look normal, after all those we killed are dead they can't tell anyone.

Come on give me your hand and let us go to bed, what's done is done.

A terrible decision was made, concerning where she was buried. She was a treasure.

A treasure to the country.
A treasure to the world,
she did no evil killing,
so please, take my word.

Imogen (aged 12)

A serial killer in her first life and a bad child of god. She was forever beating and ordering her children, her husband Macbeth and her servants.

Goodbye to an unwanted human

Lewis (aged 12)

HOW SHOULD THE QUEEN BE BURIED?

- At the end of the ceremony, step forward in role as the Lord High Sheriff to ask what is to be done with the body of Lady Macbeth? In doing so you are setting the scene to immediately after the battle. Urge King Malcolm to treat her remains with honour and justice, but go on to say, that because of the many rumours and stories circulating about her alleged involvement with the murders in her husband's reign, it is vital to establish the truth. You are sure, that the new King, would wish to bring in an era of justice and respect for the truth. Also raise the issue of Lady Macbeth's burial, for if she is innocent of the allegations, then she should be given the Christian burial a queen deserves. If she is guilty of the crimes, then her remains should be placed in an unmarked grave in unconsecrated ground.

- Call upon the King to set up a Royal Commission, composed of himself and the nobles of Scotland, to hear witnesses and decide the truth. Ask for the general approval of your proposal. Discuss with the nobles who should be called upon, as character witnesses. Request the King guarantees immunity to anyone who talks to the Commission.

- Ask the children to role-play a conversation between two nobles on their way to collect their hawks to go hunting, in which they are discussing the rumours and gossip which abound about Lady Macbeth.

- With the children out of role, generate a written list of all the people who had contact with Lady Macbeth during her life, briefly discussing the kind of contact they had had with her. Divide the list into two; characters from the play, and 'extras', or those whom the children identify, who don't appear in the play. Make sure that those who would have known her well, such as her parents, and the circle of friends and acquaintances from her early life are included. If it does not arise, suggest she has surviving children, brothers and sisters and servants such as a handmaid, who can be included.

- Ask each child to choose a role from the list, which they think they can sustain, and ensure that there is at least one role for each of the different kinds of people associated with her private life. Include the Doctor from the actual play, amongst them, and ensure there are sufficient children to be nobles, three or four perhaps, who sit with the King and yourself as the Commission, to ask questions and make the final judgement.

- Conclude this vital part of the preparation by going over the list and placing individuals as either for and against Lady Macbeth. Suggest to them that their evidence will need to include at least an anecdote, which illustrates why they hold a particular opinion of her. In the capacity of Lord High Sheriff, you can steer the drama if necessary.

Conflicts and Tensions: Developing the Drama

THE ROYAL COMMISSION HEARS EVIDENCE

- It is important that you allow the children time to prepare what it is they wish to say at the Commission, in the role they have chosen, or to devise questions they will put to witnesses, in role as one of the nobles on the Commission. The members of the Commission will need to ask questions, which establish the incidents of the play, and reveal the reactions of those involved at the time, they can also question the 'extras' in the manner of barristers, examining witnesses. Point out to them, the importance of first hand evidence, in particular the exact words a person said, this gives weight to Lady Macbeth's actual speeches in the play. Give the Doctor, or any character who might have overheard her or talked to her, transcripts of her speeches, and ask them to present these at the hearing as evidence of her state of mind. This preparation may well be in pairs, allowing for rehearsal and the consolidation of ideas.

- Arrange the drama space appropriately for the Commission, ensuring that the King has a prominent position.

- Begin the Commission with either the King or yourself, reminding everyone of the need to establish where Lady Macbeth should be laid to rest.

- Call each witness to the front and ask them to state who they are, how they knew Lady Macbeth, and then swear them in. Invite the nobles to put questions to them. Each person will need to establish the credibility of their evidence, but in the challenges to their comments, you as the Lord High Sheriff will need to exercise discretion, to avoid cross examination which shifts the attention from the Queen. However, challenges to verify and establish claims are quite in order.

- Ask those who knew her, such as her handmaid and the Doctor to present to the Commisssion, paraphrases of her speeches. These can be used by quoting from them or given out as written records of her words.

- Between hearings of evidence, out of their role, the children could compose letters she might have written, from which extracts could be read to the Commission. The Doctor who witnessed her sleep walking and over-heard her guilt-ridden monologues, could compose some writing, and offer his views on her state of mind.

- Ask the class, through small group improvisation or paired role play, to reconstruct flashbacks of some of the incidents mentioned in the Commission, whether they are part of the play or 'additional memories' of the participants. This will add variety to their engagement, and might include a reconstruction of her death, a conversation with a servant or a nobleman when Duncan's body was found, or her instructions to the night porter on the eve of the King's murder. Alternatively, groups could show the incident which finally tips her over into madness.

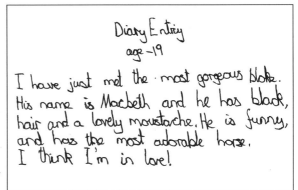

Diary Entry
age ~19

I have just met the most gorgeous bloke. His name is Macbeth and he has black, hair and a lovely moustache. He is funny, and has the most adorable horse. I think I'm in love!

Lisa (aged 12)

A DEEPER UNDERSTANDING: HER CHILDHOOD

- In role as the Lord High Sheriff, re-establish the Commission and call upon those characters who have not yet volunteered. These might include members of her family or childhood friends, as well as people with 'axes to grind' including perhaps the three witches, or Hecate, through the agency of a medium. Their evidence might include earlier incidents in her life, such as her reactions to Macbeth when she first met him. If this proves too demanding, discuss with the class possible influences upon her life and events in her childhood.

- Ask the children to portray some of these as small group improvisations, in the manner of the re-constructions in TV *Crime-Watch* style programmes.

- Ask the class who they would like to hot seat, Lady Macbeth or Macbeth himself in order to

gain added insight into their personal attitudes, feelings, and motives. You, or an able child, might take up the role.

- Ask the class to write an entry Lady Macbeth made in her diary, either in her childhood or at some later point in her life.

- The moral climate that Macbeth had created, could also be explored through the lives and testimonies of the murderers that he employed. These criminals were probably well known to the authorities and their past lives and records could be invented through improvisation. This is an opportunity to include details from the social history of Tudor and Jacobean times.

Resolutions: Drawing the Drama Together

THE KING AND THE NOBLES DECIDE

- Set up the Commission again and in role as the Lord High Sheriff summarise the evidence, particularly as it relates to Lady Macbeth. Clarify any details and direct the nobles to consider the evidence they've heard, and to form an opinion about her as a person, and her role in the crimes which the play portrayed.

- Ask the children in groups to consider their feelings about her, both in role and as themselves. Ask them to combine these into one written group statement, which someone can then read to the Commission.

- In role as the Lord High Sheriff, confer briefly with the King, in front of the class, agree the majority opinion, and pass judgement upon where she is to be buried.

R.I.P.
God forgive
a sorry soul
a tragic end
a life of hell
a life forgotten
An awful way to die.

Rory (aged 13)

- Ask the class individually to write an epitaph about Lady Macbeth or a longer obituary if appropriate, regardless of the decision about her. These could be swapped around and some read out loud.

- Out of role, reflect together upon the issues in the drama and how they related to the themes of the play. Also, consider the children's understanding of being in the process of drama, and how the use of different conventions allowed a varied and more complex appreciation of Lady Macbeth to develop.

Extension Activities

- Create other omens for the play and express them in Shakespearean language. These could be written up as proverbs or placed as additional script in the context of the play.

- Create small group improvisations of events, which might reasonably have been in the play. For example: the first contact Macbeth has with the murderers of Macduff; the meeting between Malcolm and the King of England, when he requests help to gain his throne back; the scene in which Macduff leaves his wife and children; or a meeting between Malcolm and the witches.

- Put the porter on the hot seat in order to reconstruct the movement of people in and out of the castle on the night of Duncan's murder.

- The Truth Commission in South Africa inspired the main dramatic form in this drama, so the events giving rise to this could be considered.

Resourcing Further Drama from Play Scripts

Classroom drama can make good use of play scripts as resources, enabling the class to elaborate upon the parameters of the text, through both enactment of the script and improvised investigation of the layers of meaning within it, as well as examining characters' motives, and moments of tension. Through such work, the children's comprehension of the play can be enriched. An initial extract of the play, describing for example, the characters and the set can be offered to a class to build an improvisation around. Alternatively, the words spoken in a particular encounter can be given to the class to use and extend through improvisation.

As in *Macbeth*, characters from the play can be identified and their earlier life examined and created in some detail, to build an understanding of their motives and later behaviour in the play. It is possible to use a range of drama conventions to explore the history of significant characters, as well as their actions and behaviour in the situations mentioned in the actual text. This can help children understand that a written script has many interpretations and possibilities. After improvising a conversation or scene, small groups can write their own section of the play script and compare this to the author's version, even perhaps producing it as part of a radio play.

We recommend in particular, the publication, *Ways with Plays* which offers both a rationale for the use of play scripts in the classroom and a reference list of plays available. It is written by Jackie Taylor, Mark Freeman and Jenny Bailey (1998) and published by Devon County Council. In relation to specific play scripts we recommend:

The Morgans Field, Berlie Doherty, Collins
This play examines Morgan's land and the various buyers who compete to purchase it. It incorporates a historical perspective on the land and offers plenty of openings for improvisational classroom drama.

The Angel of Nitshill Rd, Anne Fine, Ginn
This is adapted from the book and allows comparisons to be made. It explores the issue of bullying, both verbal and physical and provides a wealth of open ended scenarios to develop in drama.

The Computer Nut, Betsy Byars, Longman
In this story, Kate the heroine, makes contact via the computer with the controller of an alien spaceship. This friendly alien enables her to learn about relationships. It suits the medium of classroom drama, since there are opportunities for investigation and extension throughout.

Changes in the Night, Heather Eyles, Longman
This intriguing play raises the question of sexual stereotyping and, as it is partly set in a Victorian context, it prompts variety and comparison with today. Some scenes might be read and others developed through classroom drama.

Bill's New Frock, Anne Fine, Longman
This is adapted from the book and aimed at 11-13 year olds, although it would also work with younger children. It explores the consequences for Bill when he wakes up one morning and finds he has turned into a girl. Drama activities and writing suggestions are also offered.

Flat Stanley, adapted by Sheila Lane and Marion Kemp from the story by Jeff Brown, Ward Lock Educational
This illustrated playscript explores Stanley's adventures and how he handles being flat. It offers the opportunity to develop new adventures for him and explore his personality and others' responses to him.

The work of William Shakespeare is worth studying for a multitude of reasons, including the role his writing played in the Jacobean period as part of the origin of modern theatre. Many plays at the time dealt with the contemporary concerns in an extreme fashion, but with extraordinarily evocative language. These plays, or extracts from them are useful resources for drama since they often explored ambitious, wilful, and murderous individuals. The Jacobean Tragedies developed many of the same issues Shakespeare had been engaged with, and we recommend Webster's, *The Duchess of Malfi* and *The White Devil*, Tourneur's, *The Revenger's Tragedy*; and Middleton and Rowley's, *The Changeling*. Modern texts dealing with the same issues can usefully be examined through drama prior to reading the play, for example, the role that fate or inevitability plays in tragedy, is central to an understanding of the period. Although the politics of the day was beginning to give men and women the power of choice and decision over their affairs, the chance factor could also be explored in biographies e.g. of Cardinal Wolsey or Lady Jane Grey.

PART

TWO

imagining
and
believing

responding
and
reflecting

Chapter 13
Planning Classroom Drama

Introduction

Classroom drama is more often than not focused upon people and relies upon their life stories, which can be fact or fiction, or a combination of both. In drama we make-believe we are other people in other places, living in other times, facing ordinary but significant human problems. So planning a single lesson or a series of drama lessons, involves a process of identifying a general area of interest, which could be drawn from across the curriculum, and the key features of a related human narrative: the people, the place they are in, and the predicament they face. The specific areas of learning and teaching objectives also need to be identified and related to this human narrative.

A wealth of resources are available which offer the teacher a basis on which to build. The re-enactment of any text is best avoided, but each text, artefact, curriculum focus or tale can be usefully employed to support planning. If you explore the gaps in a text, or seek to investigate the history of an artefact, or co-author a new tale, then the drama remains open-ended and can harness the children's imaginations, whilst still responding to the chosen areas of learning.

When the general focus, the narrative elements and the specific learning areas, have been identified, then an actual session can be mapped out. This map will include a series of dramatic activities which enable the children to step into the imaginary world, focus upon certain tensions and conflicts in it and seek to resolve these and reflect upon them. So each drama session can usefully be divided into three major sections.

- *First Encounters: Creating the Drama Context.* This involves introducing and establishing the narrative elements of people, place and predicament.
- *Conflicts and Tensions: Developing the Drama.* This involves focusing upon and investigating the major dramatic tension and learning areas.
- *Resolutions: Drawing the Drama Together.* This involves harnessing the children's ideas and insights, shaping the culmination to the fiction, and reflecting upon the learning involved.

Follow up/work or extension activities outside the dramatic context, may also be planned to summarise or extend the children's learning. The actual map of the drama session offers you, the teacher, considerable structural security and should allow you to feel safe since you will have anticipated some of the responses to the tensions. However, teaching is not a science or a manufacturing process. You will need to keep an open and flexible attitude towards your plan, and exercise your professional judgement about when to follow it and when to re-organise it in the light of the children's responses during the drama. If the plan is adhered to during the first session, the following session could build upon the class's expressed interests or be planned in response to your assessment of their learning. Occasionally, you may completely refocus the session allowing the children to lead the drama in an unexpected direction. Overall however, you retain considerable responsibility for what takes place and must seek both to guide the children towards particular activities and teaching/learning objectives as well as respond to their questions and interests by integrating these into your sessions.

In the secondary school, your planning will need to take account of the children's increasing ability to deal with issues and situations which are more complex and frequently ambiguous, indeed even contradictory, as in the drama about the Rainforest (chapter 6). Older children also need to examine social issues which are relevant to their own interests, the development of their identity, and the pressures they encounter, as well as those which expand their interests beyond their immediate family.

The Planning Process

```
┌─────────────────────────────────────────────────────────────┐
│                   GENERAL AREA OF FOCUS                      │
└─────────────────────────────────────────────────────────────┘
```

TEACHING OBJECTIVES AND LEARNING AREAS	RESOURCING THE NARRATIVE
• The Imagination	• People
• Personal and Social Skills	• Place
• The Drama Processes	• Predicament
• Language	
• Reflection	
• Content of the Drama	

```
┌─────────────────────────────────────────────────────────────┐
│              PRIOR EXPERIENCE AND MATERIALS                  │
└─────────────────────────────────────────────────────────────┘
```

MAPPING THE DRAMA OUT

- First Encounters: Creating the Drama Context

- Conflicts and Tensions: Developing the Drama

- Resolutions: Drawing the Drama Together

```
┌─────────────────────────────────────────────────────────────┐
│                   EXTENSION ACTIVITIES                       │
└─────────────────────────────────────────────────────────────┘
```

Additionally, Year 8 & 9 children will be considering drama as an exam option, so a slightly greater element of performance will lead into the theatrical aspects of drama, and the awareness and knowledge of different styles of theatre which is a part of GCSE studies. With this in mind you may like to use play scripts in the manner we suggest in Macbeth (chapter 12). However, alongside this move to introduce knowledge and experience of drama as an established art form, the education of the children's personal and social skills, and their powers of communication and imagination, should be maintained. The pursuit of interpreting a playwright's intentions, which is a valid part of the drama exam curriculum should not dominate the broader learning you are seeking to encourage. The planning process for classroom drama remains constant in both key stages.

A   A General Area of Focus

The drama will be linked to a general learning area within the curriculum, so the planning process will often begin with a current topic or theme. For example, if you are focusing upon the Victorians, this might prompt you into planning a drama about Victorian children or Dr Barnardo. If you are focusing on traditional tales you might e.g. use a short story from Alexander McCall Smith's (1989) collection *Children of Wax*. It may be that citizenship is your chosen curriculum focus in which case the drama might explore a local planning issue or an environmental concern.

B   Teaching Objectives and Learning Areas.

Explicit teaching objectives encourage the teacher to keep the session focused. The teaching objectives need to be identified and carefully integrated into the plan when mapping out the session. This will ensure that the children's attainment in these areas is visible and that the teacher can judge the extent to which learning has taken place and which particular areas need further development.

The source of the teaching objectives are the six areas of learning in drama, these all interrelate and are dependent upon one another, for instance, empathy is an act of the imagination, as well as a developing personal outlook. They are separated for the purpose of planning and assessment, see Chapter 14 for an elaboration of these. The learning areas include:

- the imagination
- personal and social skills
- the drama processes
- language
- reflection
- the content of the drama

Practically, it is only possible to select two or three learning areas and devise related teaching objectives to focus upon in any given drama session, in response to the children's needs, the narrative elements and the general area of focus. Over time the tailored teaching objectives need to reflect all six areas of learning in drama. For example, in planning a lesson around Tennyson's *'The Lady of Shalott'*, the teacher may decide to work upon the imagination, and personal and social skills, as well as their ability to interpret the language of the poem and draw out meaning. So the specific teaching objectives and learning areas of this drama might include the following, (the learning areas are in italics);

- generate original and effective ideas in the context of the drama (*the imagination*).
- tolerate the ambiguity and uncertainty, in both the content and process of this drama (*personal and social skills*).
- writing in role, displaying empathy and insight (*language*).

Alongside the tailored teaching objectives, many other learning opportunities exist because of the all embracing nature of drama. Teachers need to seek a balance in relation to the planned objectives and the unplanned learning opportunities that may emerge. Experience certainly shows that to ignore the children's interest all the time, risks turning drama into an entirely teacher directed activity, and losing the children's creativity and commitment. It also fails to develop their independence in drama.

C   Resourcing the Narrative: People, Place and Predicament

The three elements of narrative; people, place and predicament are the basic components around which, individual drama sessions can be mapped. As the planning diagram indicates these are chosen alongside the learning areas, but must be selected before the dramatic action can be mapped out. *A variety of resources* can be used to help plan the people, place and predicament in the drama. Teachers do not need to create these narrative elements themselves, but can turn to novels, short story collections, traditional tales, folk and fairy tales, myths, legends and faith tales, all of which contain these elements. Real life sources can also be used, such as newspaper reports, letters, historical documents eg; diaries, eyewitness accounts, and the facsimiles of official documents, such as the Magna Carta. However, these do not represent the only resources, visuals of all kinds also offer starting points, for example: paintings and sculpture, photographs and comic strips, TV extracts and artefacts, as well as illustrations from picture books and individual poems. At the planning stage, for instance, a painting of a child might prompt the teacher to consider the character who is portrayed (e.g. who is she, what's she feeling, why does she look uncertain), then decide upon a place for the drama (e.g. a pier) and a predicament (e.g. she is considering running away from home). Drama can also be resourced by selecting one or more of the narrative elements from visual, musical or poetic resources and then inventing the remaining elements in response to these.

The life stories of historically significant people also lend themselves to the planning process, although only one aspect of their life is needed for a drama. This will not involve historical re-enactment but may focus, for example, on an in-depth examination of Sir Walter Raleigh's chequered and entrepreneurial career. In addition, scientific and geographical themes can also be used as a source base. For example, in a drama based upon pollution, the place could be a shanty town in the Third World next to a chemical plant, the people, those dwelling nearby, and the predicament: the emission of strong fumes and gases from the industrial plant at night.

In the secondary school, awareness of the current curriculum foci, and liaison with other departments will increase the likelihood of enhancing children's learning across the curriculum. Their knowledge of the content area, will deepen their involvement and is likely to strengthen their commitment to the drama.

In using various resources to establish the people, place and predicament of the drama, you may also wish to integrate the resource into the actual drama. For example, by reading an extract from the chosen poem during the drama or by showing the photograph or artefact to the class. Depending on the maturity and experience of the class, you can actually involve them in the planning process so that their ideas contribute to the initial mapping out of the narrative elements.

1   PEOPLE

The roles children are given or adopt in classroom drama have a marked influence on their possible learning. Children need to know who they are, before they can react with ease and authenticity in drama, so their initial forays into role will be more successful if the roles selected are fairly close to their own experience. For example in chapter 2, Creating a Local Museum, the children use their interests and local knowledge to establish a museum for their area. Whilst in chapter 11, Anne Frank, they are put in the position of Jews in World War Two, and in chapter 6, The Rainforest, they are also in markedly different roles as the slum-dwellers of Sao Paulo and then as tribes-people of the Amazon Rainforest. With increasing age and experience, children develop the ability to use roles which are more distant and dissonant from themselves.

In selecting various roles for the children, you'll need to identify the kind of characters likely to be found in a particular place and take into account the children's age and experience, being prepared to challenge the children to adopt several roles. Switching from one role to another during the drama, has many advantages and offers potentially richer learning, through providing several perspectives on an issue. However, it can be confusing and may result in affirming superficial stereotypes if not handled carefully. A full representation of the different roles, and views needs to be articulated, or stereotypes challenged in the reflection period or in the extension activities following the drama.

The historical time frame of the drama will also influence the roles adopted, in which case it may be that the children will benefit from undertaking some background research prior to the drama, but they will need to make the roles their own. You may have to extend some licence towards their interpretation of the facts, which you can address during your reflection time, if you consider the accepted historical line has been grossly disturbed.

The role children adopt is the perspective from which they learn; so you'll need to select characters whose predicaments and experiences will enable your selected learning areas to be examined. By working through different roles yourself, you can extend their role repertoire, simultaneously challenging them to take up a range of roles associated with your role. Consequently, careful thought needs to be given to the teacher's many roles at the planning stage.

2   PLACE

Drama has to happen somewhere and since it is only through the imagination that drama takes place at all, it is clear that visualising/creating the place in which the drama is going to take place is an important preliminary activity. The place or setting will also influence the kind of characters who could inhabit the story, and the conflicts and tensions which might arise. It is not that the children become the forest and the trees, but that in exploring the forest together they build their sense of this imaginary place. For example in Anne Frank, the children consider and create the spice factory in which the Franks hide, before experiencing the threat of the Nazis in this context. In selecting the place in which the drama operates the teacher needs to find a suitable venue which will enable the learning areas to be developed. In addition a balance needs to be established over time between the following

- *Everyday examples*: such as a prison, a factory or a station.
- *Idealised examples*: such as the castle, the desert or outer space.
- *Fictional examples*: such as the farmhouse of *Animal Farm*, the island of *Lord of the Flies*, or the village in *Goodnight Mr Tom*.

A role-play area, with its cross curricular connections can occasionally be established and related to the venue of the drama, to promote further investigation and research. This works particularly well when the place for the unfolding classroom drama remains constant for several weeks, so the work in one context feeds work in the other. In the secondary school, continuity will often be through the agency of the teacher in role, representing the place, where the action happens, e.g. as a Station-master or the Captain of the ship. Alternatively the use of symbols or objects, which represent the place, e.g. a coats of arms of the landowner, upon whose land the drama takes place, or the tankard from the Inn in which the murder takes place can be useful.

3   PREDICAMENT

Without experiencing a genuine sense of conflict or tension, through their engagement in role in the imaginary situations there would be no drama. The children may initially be interested in the people and keen to build a sense of place, but it is through their response to the predicament that their commitment deepens and they feel and experience the drama as real.

Dramatic conflicts or tensions trigger the 'electricity' of drama, because they involve some element of anticipation, a sense of waiting, or uncertainty in relation to some unresolved situation. A variety of tensions and predicaments exist in life and fiction and you'll need to select one which suits your class and your chosen learning areas. Predicaments may relate to any of the following tensions:

- *challenges* - obstacles which need to be overcome.
- *limitations* - factors which inhibit or constrain the intended direction of events.
- *decisions* - the pros and cons of the situation which have to be assessed.
- *destiny* - the influence of chance or fate as well as fixed social or moral expectations.
- *changes* - alterations to the status quo which produce new predicaments and tensions.
- *ignorance* - being unaware of significant factors which cause difficulties.
- *waiting* - this often heralds change and challenge, as well as compounding stress.
- *misunderstanding* - mismatches and misreading situations can bring conflict.

Predicaments in classroom drama demand the children's involvement, and require them to respond to the situation in which they find themselves, without knowing where it will lead. So the predicament forms the dynamo to drama, the personal commitment and affective involvement which enables children to learn from living and feeling inside the drama.

D   Prior Experience and Materials

Once the narrative structure of people, place, predicament has been resourced and the learning areas identified, the teacher can discern what experiences would be preferable for the children to have undertaken prior to the drama. In many cases, no specific previous experience will be necessary, in others if you are integrating the drama into an area of the curriculum, you'll need to carefully consider where to place the drama sessions in your medium term plan. Any materials needed can be noted in the plan.

E   Mapping Out the Drama Sessions

Using the ideas for people, place and predicament, the teacher can map out an extended sequence of activities which constitute the drama session. A range of drama conventions will be employed to investigate the issues and respond to the specific teaching objectives and learning areas identified. Each session can be divided into three sections; first encounters, conflicts and tensions and finally resolutions.

1. FIRST ENCOUNTERS: CREATING THE DRAMA CONTEXT.

This phase of your drama establishes two essentials. Firstly, it needs to 'hook' the children's interest, which is the responsive side of the imagination, and the basic motivation for their involvement and subsequent learning. Secondly, it needs to establish the world in which the drama takes place, through the elements of people, place and predicament. It is the predicament, which is the primary initiator of the drama, as it is the children's response to this which becomes the thoughts and actions of the drama.

Your initial drama strategy needs to open intriguing 'doors' for the class, to generate involvement and create interest. Lengthy class discussions need to be avoided at this juncture, rather the children's ideas need to be encouraged through *early imaginative activity*. The resource chapters utilise a wide range of strategies to spark interest and establish a framework on which the drama can build. The resource itself may provide an initial prompt, for example the poem in *The Highwayman* (chapter 10), or part of a novel may be told or read, as in *The Angel of Nitshill Road* (chapter 5). These begin to offer information about imaginative contexts to which the children can respond. There are many other ways to step into the world of drama which work well with children, since they appeal to their sense of adventure and prompt their imagination to produce ideas, and the actions and visual images which accompany them.

Many drama teachers suggest that the most powerful way of engaging children is by using the medium itself, through *the teacher in role* as a primary shaping force presenting the predicament to the children, as in Moses in the Bullrushes, (chapter 8). Real people, particularly when they are 'unknown' to the children, generate an initial and compelling interest. Their three dimensional nature seems to demand attention, and if you use this and manipulate your role, you can present the predicament which you embody so that the children take it on themselves. Also, because you are involved in the drama, the children will follow you into the situation, you are the model for their participation. In other words, if you do it, they'll do it! In addition you're able to address their tentative questions and comments from within the drama, which helps them orientate themselves to the situation and begin to make sense of it. The longer you sustain the role with their full attention, the more deeply they'll become involved. Another strategy to engage the children is to use narration, and become the *storyteller*. Through your language you can evoke atmosphere and tension and help the children create visual images. In this way you can pass on information, which builds the context and background about the people and the impending predicament.

Various kinds of 'magic' are also useful, with the younger end of this age range, as initial strategies which facilitate *imaginative* access to other worlds. With older children, the power of magic diminishes and turns into superstition, so alternatives need to be employed. Visualising an imaginary place, conjecturing about it, and then rearranging the space together, and placing imaginary things in it, even making a corporate map, can help them build a mental picture of the place and the people who might inhabit it. Objects which have strong associations, or imply another place, such as a key or a ticket, also allow an easy mental connection to a dramatic situation. Similarly, the discovery of intriguing unfinished messages, or things which are out of place such as a full bag of shopping unattended on a country road act as invitations to find out more. The deliberate use of sci-fi scenarios, as in the film *The Matrix*, is a well accepted convention which automatically gives access to other worlds and the 'paranormal'. If they are used however, the human issues within them need to become the primary focus of your teaching. The danger is that the sensational aspects serve to overwhelm the ordinary, but profound understanding which you are trying to explore.

These first encounters need to help children establish a strong sense of the place and themselves as people, so that when they encounter predicaments they can respond quickly and become committed to resolving the conflict. Their imaginations need to be triggered into action through early mental and physical engagement in the fictional world.

2. CONFLICTS AND TENSIONS: DEVELOPING THE DRAMA

As the drama with its incidents unfolds, the dramatic tension increasingly holds the children's attention, and opens up the themes, which will be used to explore the learning areas. During this time the class become more involved in the issues beneath the narrative they are creating. At first their imaginary world may be somewhat superficial and oriented towards enthusiastic dramatic action, but with your guidance and through your selection of appropriate drama conventions, their work will grow in depth and insight. Later, through creating and reflecting upon this imaginary world, the children come to understand themselves and the real world in which they live, because the drama world is an analogy for the real world.

The range of drama conventions and symbols planned in this section need to keep the drama moving and ensure variety and pace, as well as provide the opportunity to investigate the learning areas. Since each convention provides particular kinds of support and shapes the drama in various ways, the children's involvement can be deepened through the use of appropriate techniques, which offer new perspectives, open up dilemmas, and examine moral choices, as well as their consequences. Once again we recommend the convention of teacher in role for its flexibility and power.

Once the class has begun to examine the issues in the narrative, their developing views and insights may prompt questions or identify areas of interest which don't coincide with your plans. Initially, it may be preferable to pursue the activities you've planned and merely log the children's particular interests in order to explore them in a future session. With experience however, you'll find you can respond to some of the children's interests and re-orient the session appropriately whilst still bearing in mind the intended learning areas.

In this phase of the drama, when the conflicts and tensions come to the fore, the class will move constantly between action and being thoughtful. They will live in the drama (eg. as they confront the surveyor in the Rainforest, chapter 6), as well as being more detached (eg. when considering the speeches of Lady Macbeth, chapter 12). These *moves between engagement and reflection* are not overtly marked, but are an integral part of your developing drama and need to be mapped into the plan. They are also mental preparations for the deeper reflection that makes up the concluding phase.

3. RESOLUTIONS: DRAWING THE DRAMA TOGETHER

In this phase of the drama the children continue to work together through action and reflection to resolve the drama predicament, reach a reasonable conclusion and then consider their learning in drama. In mapping out this part of the drama, the teacher can focus more explicitly upon the learning areas and issues to be examined as the fictional world closes. Once some form of resolution has been established, techniques which help children *express the insights gained* through the drama can be employed. This may well involve discussion, drawing or shared writing to summarise the views, positions, themes and morals examined. *Making connections* will be a central focus at this time, whether these are personal parallels, connections to particular characters or themes in well known class texts or wider connections in relation to their school, home, community and the wider world. The diversity of insights gained need to be articulated, shared and valued.

This phase of the drama should offer the children the space and time to digest the dramatic experience and revisit some of the learning areas. The teacher may focus on different learning areas over time, so that, for example, on some occasions the curriculum content will be profiled in this part, whilst on others, the drama process and the conventions used, will be discussed, in still others, the personal and social issues may be foregrounded in this drawing together time. This time also provides the teacher with the opportunity to offer *explicit feedback* to the class and to assess their understanding at the close of the drama.

F   Extension Activities

As the drama draws to a close the teacher will be gauging the appropriateness of various pre-planned extension activities, based partly on an assessment of the children's learning. Activities across the whole breadth of the curriculum can be undertaken, although tenuous links need to be avoided and those activities which respond to the children's expressed interests during the drama, and which continue to pursue the learning areas should take preference. Such work has the potential to build on the insights gained, revisit the issues examined and give extended voice to the responses generated. The class could be invited to join the teacher in generating their own list of possible activities. These might include retelling sections of the tale on tape, creating storyboards, writing play scripts or scenes, making posters to advertise the film version, producing newspaper articles, writing in role as one of the characters, or co-authoring a class book. In the secondary school, unless a co-ordinated curriculum has been established, the extension activities are likely to be mainly language based, often shaped by the timetable and the teacher's individual interests, responsibilities and focus.

A PLANNING CHECKLIST

Having identified the teaching objectives/learning areas, resourced the narrative elements and created a map of your session, including first encounters, conflicts and tensions as well as resolutions, you would be well advised to read through your plan. A number of points are worth considering, these include:

1. What is the early narrative hook to invite the learners into the imaginative world?

2. Are a variety of drama conventions employed to investigate the issue?

3. Does the sequence of activities provide a varied pace and rhythm, so that there are moments of relative stillness and focused reflection, as well as times of more active energetic engagement?

4. Are the teaching objectives/learning areas woven into the fabric of the lesson? Can they be evidenced in action and reflection through the spoken and written word, in particular in the resolutions section?

5. Is there a reasonable balance between pair, small group and whole class work over the lesson?

6. Are the planned roles and activities appropriate to the children's age, experience and ability?

7. Are there any children for whom the themes, issues or objectives are likely to be very challenging? What can be planned to help these individuals?

talking
and
writing

Chapter 14
ASSESSING CLASSROOM DRAMA

Introduction

The National Curriculum requirements for drama focus upon the three strands of arts education: making, performing and responding. These are useful and prompt a breadth of drama activities, but do not constitute sufficiently focused areas for assessing children's learning in drama. In the National Curriculum, drama is placed within English in the programme of study for Speaking and Listening, but to limit ourselves to merely assessing this aspect of drama would be to ignore its contribution to other areas of learning. Classroom drama involves developing six areas of learning simultaneously. These areas interrelate, are dependent upon one another and shift in significance at different moments in a drama. As children make, perform and respond in classroom drama, there are many opportunities for developing their learning in all of these areas.

Learning Areas in Drama

- The Imagination
- Personal and Social Skills
- The Drama Processes
- Language
- Reflection
- The Content of the Drama

Progression and development in each of the learning areas is related to children's growing independence and ability to work in depth, examining increasingly complex issues and taking more control of conventions to achieve their desired ends. The individual strands of progression listed below extend those identified in our book, **Resourcing Drama 5-8.** However, if a class is inexperienced in drama then some of the stages of progression identified in that text, may more appropriately describe their development.

The Imagination

Classroom drama relies primarily upon the imagination and provides rich opportunities for its development, through refining and enhancing established ideas, as well as producing new and original ones. Progression in imaginative development in drama will involve children in:

- Offering ideas originating from personal feelings, values, experience or knowledge.
- Developing increasingly effective, original, clear and vivid ideas.
- Consciously generating ideas to develop the drama.
- Controlling and manipulating both spontaneous and considered ideas to fit the fictional situation.
- Developing and showing empathy in the construction and portrayal of the drama.
- Consciously shaping the dramatic space and deliberately placing objects and roles within it.
- Developing the ability to maintain different roles during an extended sequence of drama.

Personal and Social Skills

Classroom drama allows children to develop their personal and social skills in secure imaginary contexts. These skills form the basis of their moral development. Progression in personal and social skills in drama will involve children in:

- Developing flexibility, an ability to negotiate with others and an awareness of the consequences of words and actions.
- Developing their confidence and independence in drama.
- Considering in increasing depth, the moral and social issues in drama.
- Engaging with their own personal feelings to shape and develop drama.
- Tolerating ambiguity and uncertainty in the drama situation and process.
- Developing a sense of detachment from the roles and tensions within drama.
- Developing and informing their personal and social identity, as well as their moral values.

The Drama Processes

Classroom drama enables children to use and understand a range of drama conventions, which allow them to explore meaning and express their ideas. Children can learn to select, manipulate and shape these conventions for themselves. Progression in using the drama process will involve children in:

- Recognising and using conventions with increasing independence.
- Suggesting and employing conventions in order to achieve their desired effects.
- Using conventions with increasing ingenuity, imagination and understanding of the art form.
- Developing an increasing range of verbal, gestural and movement skills.
- Maintaining and developing roles/characters, situations/plots, and contrasts/tensions.
- Articulating and discussing the use of the drama process and its conventions.
- Using a critical language in drama, which enables contrasts and comparisons to be made in their own work and that of others.

Language

Classroom drama fosters a wide range of spoken and written language registers through the variety of roles adopted and can also foster an interest in texts and a closer examination of them, for drama is inference in action. Progression in language development in drama will involve children in:

* Using an increasingly wide range of spoken and written language registers.
* Selecting appropriate and effective language in role according to purpose, context and audience.
* Using subtle intonation patterns, and appropriate volume and tenor to express feelings and communicate information.
* Developing increasing empathy and insight expressed in writing from a particular stance.
* Developing enhanced understanding of a written text through the drama investigation and active reading.
* Employing a critical and reflective language to respond to and evaluate drama.

Reflection

In classroom drama, children both live within a fictional context to make meanings and step outside of it to reflect upon the unfolding drama. They also make connections between the real world and the imaginary one. Through this process, children develop their reflective capacity and ability to evaluate their drama, as well as develop their knowledge of the world. Progression in reflective development in drama will involve children in:

* Developing a capacity to view situations from differing perspectives.
* Making connections between the drama and the real world.
* Developing an increasing ability to identify and understand parallel situations.
* Recognising patterns and similarities between drama sessions, both in content and in the process.
* Distinguishing between personal feelings and values, and those of the role in drama.
* Articulating views of each other's contributions showing tolerance, acceptance, appreciation and enjoyment.

The Content of the Drama

The content of each classroom drama is related to an area of the curriculum and enables the children to develop, use and refine their knowledge in this area. In developing their ability to handle the content, children will be involved in:

* Exploring their knowledge and understanding of the content.
* Developing their knowledge and understanding of the content gained from different perspectives.
* Recognising influences, crucial factors, and/or turning points in the content frame of the drama.
* Discussing the issues as they relate both to real life and the fictional context of the drama.
* Suggesting and integrating varied factual knowledge with increasing accuracy and understanding.

How to Assess Classroom Drama

Assessment in classroom drama is the same as effective assessment elsewhere; it is formative and aids development, and is not merely to record activity and the children's progress. Through evaluating their engagement, as well assessing individual children's learning, you will be able to identify particular objectives for the next session, based on need and in response to the class as well as the curriculum. Whilst all six areas of learning in drama will develop simultaneously, for planning and assessment purposes it is preferable to identify only three areas to focus upon in any given session. The specific teaching objectives will be developed from these areas, (see chapter 13).

Evidence of children's learning in drama can be collected through a variety of means. These include:

- observation notes made by the teacher (during the drama or soon after)
- verbatim quotes made by the teacher (during the drama)
- drawing in role (during the drama)
- writing in role (during or after the drama)
- brief audio taped extracts (during the drama or as part of follow up work)
- photographs (also for display purposes)
- extension activities (after the drama)
- self assessment activities (after the drama)

Since it is impossible to assess and record the whole class's learning in a single session, we advise choosing small groups of children to assess in each session, ensuring whole class assessment over time. By focusing on only two or three children in each session, it is feasible to collect evidence of their learning in relation to the learning areas previously identified. For example, notes in the form of verbatim quotes and comments upon the use of their imagination, awareness of the drama process and ability to reflect, may be recorded this term. Whilst next term, a couple of pieces of writing in role, and observation notes could be used as evidence of their learning about the content and in relation to their progression in language development and personal and social skills. It is also worthwhile noting any drama contributions which you recognise as exceptional or significant for a particular child. Annual summative reporting may be short, but can reassure parents about learning in drama and offer evidence of their child's progression and development.

The quality of the children's engagement can only be evaluated at the time. You know your children and will be able to judge the level of their engagement, what they are feeling, and their attitude and involvement. Playing, when important relationships and puzzling events are explored, can be a very serious business and this is frequently evident in drama. So even when the outward appearance of the children's behaviour seems to express frivolity, their eyes may be very intent upon what is happening. At other times, powerful emotions such as outrage or anger may be clearly seen, or their feelings may be cooler, and closer to concentration and serious attention. The content of your drama will obviously have a strong bearing upon the kind of engagement the children develop. This is part of the personal and social area of learning and is directly concerned with the education of the sensibilities and feelings. Drama allows, even encourages the arousal of feelings, and enables the learner to experience and recognise these, beginning to come to a personal understanding of them. In evaluating the children's involvement as well as their learning in drama you will also be subtly assessing the quality of your session in more depth.

Chapter 15
MANAGING CLASSROOM DRAMA

INTRODUCTION

Drama is a powerful, motivating tool for learning, but many teachers lack the confidence to use it, and feel they are not theatrical enough, or are daunted by the challenge of handling children in open-ended, improvisational contexts. This chapter seeks to respond to questions teachers have asked us over the years, related to their concerns about managing classroom drama, including: maintaining control, establishing noise levels, deciding where to teach it, taking up a role, supporting shy children and dealing with difficult ones. It also discusses introducing drama to beginners, developing a positive attitude to it, fitting it into a crowded curriculum, slowing the action down and handling sensitive issues.

Do I have to act?

Drama is commonly associated with acting, with the theatre and putting on a show, so some teachers fear they need to have performance skills to do it. This is not necessary: teaching classroom drama is about developing children's understanding of themselves and the world, as well as their communication skills, so neither you, nor the children need to be actors. You will have to take up different roles, but quietness and commitment are far more effective than any kind of histrionics.

Taking on teacher in role for the first time can be a little daunting, but remember not to act, just adopt the role, believe in the situation and speak seriously and with conviction from your imagined position. You already take on a multitude of different roles in life: as a sympathetic adult; an encouraging teacher; an exasperated parent and so forth. In classroom drama you'll simply be adopting other roles to help the children learn. Try to keep in role during drama time, since if you break it briefly with a knowing smile, the children will respond to you as their teacher, rather than respond to you in role. During the drama you will be moving in and out of role, so you will not be sustaining the role for a lengthy period of time unless you and the children are very experienced. The authentic commitment, which you demonstrate through teacher in role, provides a model for the children and prompts them to take a full part in the shared endeavour.

With a class who have only a limited experience of classroom drama it would be advisable to prepare them for you going into role. Explain, for example, that you're going to walk towards the door and when you turn around and return, you'll be in role as the police superintendent. Initially, you might select high profile or more controlling roles for yourself until you feel ready to take a more vulnerable role. All roles however offer you the chance to make suggestions, ask questions and shape the unfolding drama. If the children are surprised by your behaviour in role (because it's different from usual) they may become giggly, but by continuing to take your role seriously they will quickly respond in kind and engage in the drama alongside you. Children's interest and motivation in drama are both very high, and they appreciate, enjoy and learn from the full involvement of their teacher.

What if I don't think I have enough imagination to teach classroom drama?

Don't worry! The chapters in this book show how a variety of resources can be relied upon to prompt the children's imaginative engagement. The teacher, in joining them on this journey shares in the process of exploration and makes use of a range of drama conventions to imaginatively investigate the issue at hand. Your imagination (which is the ability to make connections between ideas in any form) is in constant use in everyday contexts, ranging from 'what can I concoct for supper from what's in the cupboard', to dealing sensitively with a child in trouble. It is a capacity we all have, although some people claim not to be imaginative, what they are probably saying is that they are not 'artistic'! Be that as it may, in classroom drama, your enthusiasm, commitment, natural imaginative capacity and preparedness to be open, to consider alternatives and try are more than sufficient to make the drama successful. Any shortcomings you feel you might have, will easily be outweighed by the children's energy and willingness to have a go.

How can I motivate the children and maintain control?

Some teachers avoid drama because they are afraid of possible discipline problems and are concerned that the children will just mess about. Quality drama demands self-discipline and concentration, careful planning and the use of simple control strategies. One of the most useful strategies is a 'stop' signal: a clap of the hands, the beat of a tambour, a hand held high above the head, or you sitting in the teacher's chair. The children should be forewarned of the signal and its purpose the first time you introduce it, and with the very youngest in this age range, they could practice their response to it in a short game. There also needs to be clear general guidance from you about the appropriate use of space and objects in drama. We recommend that nothing is used by the children except their imagination, and perhaps occasionally, simple pieces of furniture.

Older children will initially need to learn the value of drama as work. Because you push the desks back or are in the hall, and are not using the conventional tools of learning, does not mean you have suspended your expectations of their behaviour. Those pupils who have experienced drama work previously, will recognise the value and the difference in this active and participatory mode of learning. Newcomers however, will need to develop a positive attitude through their engagement in the drama and through your participation and reflection both in and out of role. The children will see what it is you are working towards and begin to model their own response upon that understanding. Try to ensure that the children leave each session with a sense of achievement, which is based upon your objectives and responses as well as their involvement.

Children become actively involved in drama, expressing themselves with enthusiasm, movement and energy. This is a significant characteristic of drama, and acknowledges the role the body plays in the generation of ideas, but needs to be balanced with reflective opportunities and moments of relative stillness. In planning the classroom drama sessions, you'll find you can harness their energy and focus their thinking by using a variety of drama conventions (see Chapter 17), which offer a balance between free movement and more static work. For example, some conventions, such as small group improvisation, offer more freedom of movement than others. The balance of the planned activities supports the teacher's control and also helps give pace and rhythm to the session.

One of the most crucial control mechanisms in drama is the teacher in role. From inside the drama, you can influence and shape the dramatic enquiry and legitimately maintain control, and help the children consider the consequences of their actions. In questioning their decisions and providing time outside the drama to consider the situation, the teacher is able to retain the reins of the drama whenever necessary. You'll gradually feel more confident in selecting particular conventions in response to the children's interests, which focus their engagement and prompt consideration of the underlying issues. For example, writing or drawing in drama can create an atmosphere of individual intent, and enable the teacher to establish a quieter more reflective mode of operation.

The choice of the subject, or content of the drama, plays a significant part in motivating the children. The older the children, the greater will be the use of social and contemporary issues. The kinds of issues that relate to the children's own search for a social identity, as well as chime in with their questions about issues of human concern, will be known to you and can therefore be woven into the drama. Younger children are fascinated by the extraordinary and the fabulous, which are of course either analogies for abiding concerns and relationships, or include examples of the experiences which humanity faces and needs to resolve. Stories, myths, legends and many other resources fall easily into these categories.

How do I recognise a positive and productive attitude?

Your drama sessions will be made up of a number of different activities and phases, which will have a different feel to them. Sometimes a reflective phase is followed by a more light hearted and humorous one, but in order to recognise positive productive attitudes and involvement, you'll need to consider the overall feel of the session, and whether there has been substantial consideration of the issues you planned to examine. In other words, have the children taken seriously what they were engaged in, and which you approved off as their teacher. In doing so, humour and playfulness are not excluded, neither is enjoyment and satisfaction, but the kind of play you are encouraging has rules and is being used for the development of understanding. Sometimes however, children use the serious business of play as a medium for egotism and inappropriate expression or they become preoccupied with just one aspect of behaviour, such as violence, so this needs to be balanced with other issues. If it is possible, turn the drama towards the consequences or the causes of these preoccupations and you will find that some of their need to express these themes will dissipate. In assessing their involvement you are looking for a feeling quality that informs you of the children's serious attention. The feeling may be quite cool such as a report given on a hot seat, or it may involve more emotional engagement, such as a remonstration with an anti-animal rights campaigner, but you will be able to see and feel the children are fully engaged. This is often accompanied by an increase in their confidence in the drama, and a deep sense of satisfaction with the activity.

How do I introduce classroom drama to children who have never done it before?

Initially you'll find it useful to ascertain your children's perceptions about drama, ask them what they think it is and what they anticipate it will involve. This will reveal their attitudes and help to explain their subsequent behaviour. Talk informally about their ideas and make it clear that drama involves thinking, imagining, understanding and learning. This explanation is also for their parents, who are likely to hear from their youngsters about their drama sessions. Share your commitment and enthusiasm, your expectation that they will enjoy it and learn from it.

Sometimes the contrast with the rest of the curriculum may make children feel that drama isn't work and that it doesn't therefore require work-like behaviour. You'll need to state that classroom drama involves thinking and believing, and although it sometimes feels like play it is really work. You'll also need to agree some simple rules with the children about stop signals, the working space, and the use of materials. It is important to ensure that all your class finishes their first drama session with a sense of achievement, feeling sure they can 'do drama.' Consequently the initial activities need to be easily manageable, for example, making a small group or whole class freeze frame of some narrative action. Allowing friends to work together in this session will ease the negotiation skills required, and your positive feedback at the close of the drama will encourage them.

Isn't classroom drama rather noisy?

Drama, the art form of social encounters, demands interaction, discussion and different kinds of verbal involvement, all of which can lead to higher than usual noise levels. For example, a class of children working out how to create their group freeze frames is bound to make more noise than normal individual or pair work. But this does not provide a licence for children to make unreasonable or unacceptable noise. Each teacher has their own noise tolerance level and taking into account the nature of each convention, the room being used and the children themselves, teachers need to establish an appropriate working volume. However, if the children are more conscious of the need to keep their noise down, than upon engaging in the drama, the learning outcomes will be limited. Classroom drama often produces humour, heightened engagement and interaction, but it should also produce careful listening and create atmosphere and tension. Excessive noise works against the build up of tension, so a reduction in noise to a working 'hub-ub' will often be necessary, and again a balance of drama conventions will provide for moments of quietness, intensity and even silence.

Do I need a lot of space to work in?

Historically, the traditional view of drama as being sister to the school play and associated with music and movement, meant that the school hall became the normal place for drama. However, there are disadvantages in using this large space, not the least of which is that the children want to use all of it and initially find it hard to resist the physical impulse to rush around or perform in it! But it does offer the freedom to move freely, and supports the generation of ideas through the use of the body.

The classroom is a viable alternative and you and the class will gain a sense of privacy and will also have immediate access to writing/drawing materials there. However, there are still classrooms that are too cramped for this kind of activity, so the decision to choose the hall or the classroom has to be taken with regard to your own circumstances. It is true, moving the classroom furniture is a chore, but the advantages of closeness and the feeling of security offset this. In fact the clutter and varied spaces left in the classroom, provide interest and different levels which can be put to good effect within the session. Also, free from the constraints of the hall timetable, teachers can make more of their own choices about when to undertake classroom drama. It can, for example, be integrated into an extended history time or used to investigate a character's past in designated literacy time. The opportunities are endless if the classroom is used and drama is tailored to fit the learning agenda of the children and the time available.

How long does a classroom drama session last?

This will depend on the age, experience and maturity of the learners, as well as the issue selected for investigation. Drama integrated into cross curricular work can fire the children's interest and encourage them to research and investigate, it might also involve considerable writing in role, map making, drawing diagrams or designing, all in the service of both drama and other areas of the curriculum. If you plan to use classroom drama for multiple ends, then the time opens up and more can be achieved.

There is no fixed time span for drama; you will need to remain sensitive to the learning involved, which may result in the session being longer or shorter than you planned. More importantly perhaps the pace of the lesson needs to allow time both to focus and intensify the children's thinking. Rushing through the plan will mean you'll miss the opportunity to slow down and examine an issue, whilst if you're preoccupied with drawing everything out of an activity, this will result in restless children. You'll need to constantly refer to their interest levels and the teaching objectives, for too much speed allows nothing to consolidate in their minds, whilst too little pace encourages the dissolution of what is forming!

How can I be sure they are working in their groups?

Your professional experience of children will tell you when they are on task, or more significantly whether the group is working well together. Each group will have a dynamic and you will need to know your children to ensure that you have the right blend of people together. It is good to move children from group to group after a number of sessions, to encourage social mixing and negotiation, but only when they are at ease with drama. When you circulate to each of the groups to offer support and clarification, you can monitor this aspect. In general, the accomplishment of social skills increases with age, and consequently you will be able to use more small group work with the older the children. However, over reliance on this technique can encourage the erroneous belief that classroom drama is about doing small group plays, rather than an active method of learning which encompasses individual, pair and whole class work in order to make meaning.

What can I do about shy children?

Classroom drama is about the generation of ideas and different imaginative possibilities, as well as their subsequent examination through action and reflection, so the skill of presenting, sharing or performing is only a part. Your comments and feedback to the class need to highlight this, to honour variety and to affirm the nature of this form of drama. Children should never be pressured into doing classroom drama. Some self-conscious children may fear being watched, mocked or bossed around by more confident peers. These difficulties are not insurmountable and ironically it is often through more drama opportunities, not less, that these very youngsters will gain in confidence. Once their experience of drama has shown them they will not be continuously watched or judged, their initial discomfort frequently eases. You could offer such children a safe role in the drama, as the official photographer of the trip perhaps, or allow them to watch the drama unfold on an imaginary TV screen. This enables them to observe but still remain part of the drama.

The composition of small groups of children needs to be given careful thought, with a variety of friendship, random and engineered groups used over time to give each child a variety of social contexts to work in. When using self-selecting groups, the less popular children can be left out so move quickly to place them in the group in which they are most likely to be accepted. Less confident children may find pair work supportive and some will need time before they feel secure with this new medium. Although it is true that many children, normally quiet in the classroom, find the imaginative context liberating and become both more confident and more vocal in drama. Teachers, if they have the opportunity of watching a visiting drama teacher, often express surprise that these children volunteer for significant roles or voice their views in whole class improvisations.

What can I do about difficult children?

Occasionally, a child who hasn't experienced much drama, seeks release in being silly, or sending up their offering, and keeps looking for opportunities to show off and make the class laugh. This is often an indication that they feel insecure in drama and support strategies will need to be offered. Try to find a theme directly related to their interests or give them a particular role in the drama and seek their advice and counsel. By ensuring they are praised and encouraged for their developing commitment, they will find increasing security in their work.

Other children, who are often essentially gregarious or assertive in nature, represent another kind of challenge, by offering an almost continuous stream of ideas and suggestions. These children are very useful as 'fall-back' initiators at times, but their constant interjections, however positive, can be difficult to handle in the moment to moment interchange of the drama. Try giving these eager leaders a role alongside you. This provides them with a distinct position, but also allows you to oversee them, and foster their contributions at particular points in the drama. The removal of a child from an activity happens no more in drama than in any other lesson, but if you need to do so, ask them to sit quietly somewhere at the edge. Through not being fully removed, they can see what they are missing and since drama is highly motivating, children quickly learn to exert more self-discipline, so they can return to be involved with their friends.

How do I engage the children's feelings?

The education of the feelings through the experience of drama is legitimate, desirable and vitally important. Real engagement in the fictional context is sought for all the class. But the depth of feeling which you allow your drama to develop (with the consequent release of emotions) has to be governed by the recognition that classroom drama involves neither counselling nor group therapy. What you are endeavouring to do is address areas of human experience which are relevant to everyone and deserve investigation. It is not the task of the drama teacher to become the therapist and set out to arouse strong feelings in a group setting. The surfacing of feelings in drama, expressed through the children's engagement, is one way of recognising the quality of drama, because it is direct evidence of the children's involvement, but an appropriate balance needs to be found between emotional engagement and emotional security.

What about emotionally sensitive issues?

A deep involvement with issues is sought in classroom drama, some of which are of a sensitive nature. Emotive subjects often relate to our relationships with other people and focus upon the very nature of being human, so they should not be avoided. But such issues invariably arouse feelings of one kind or another, and you will need to watch for any effects upon the children, to protect them from personally negative feelings. Very occasionally, as a result of an associated personal experience, a child may be unable to control strong emotions. This is rare however, because in constantly moving in and out of classroom drama, the children develop a sense of 'this is drama time', and know they have one foot in the reality of the classroom. The very strength of drama is that it engages real feelings and emotions in safe, fictional contexts where these can be genuinely encountered and considered. In this way, children come to learn more about themselves and the real world and explore difficult issues in protected imaginary contexts. But do be ready to offer strategies such as drawing or private writing, and even physical games entailing laughter and contact, which can help to calm the situation and manage their emotional response. Older children are more likely to feel emotions arriving and may seek to disguise their engagement with behaviour, which retreats from the situation, such as turning it all into a joke. Humour and laughter are relaxers and releasers of tension, so they can be usefully employed by you and the children, using your professional judgement.

What can I do when there are too many ideas to incorporate?

Drama generates many ideas and possibilities which the children are eager to share, for their suggestions shape the drama and in doing so extend their understanding. Frequently, several of their different ideas could be developed and the class may need, with your advice, to decide upon which aspect they wish to take forward. You can make the decision yourself for professional reasons, although with older children prioritising and voting are often employed. Later in the drama, you could try to incorporate their different ideas into some narration and so honour the suggestions which were not taken up, or revisit these in the reflection phase. In extension work too, some children may want to return to their earlier ideas to explore them further. In drama, one of your aims is to allow a diversity of ideas to be generated, but it is also necessary to negotiate and accept collective decisions about actions and the direction of events, so that a corporate ownership of the drama develops. Part of your responsibility therefore, is to manage a fair distribution of responsibility and leadership as the drama develops.

How can I slow the action down?

Young children are often full of ideas and enthusiasm for life, and in classroom drama this can be tapped. Children enjoy the action and living in the moment and frequently want to solve the problems quickly, unravel the 'mystery' and rush on to reach some form of closure in the narrative. Classroom drama however, involves both engagement and reflection and the teacher will want to help the class consider the implications of their actions, and understand character's motives, their inner feelings and the issues at the heart of the drama. Providing time for reflection is essential throughout classroom drama, as it prompts children to make connections and consider the issues more fully on their drama journeys.

Certain drama conventions are more reflective in nature and can be useful to slow the action down, particularly when the children are losing their concentration or are over excited. When this happens, either use teacher in role in order to refocus their attention, or channel the energy being expressed in excitement, into some individual task that draws upon their thinking. This could involve writing letters or notes in role, or drawing and creating maps and diagrams. In planning the session try to create a varied pace, with activities which demand quiet stillness, concentration and reflection as well as those which demand energy, action, conversation and movement. Avoid building dramas upon action alone, and include the action of intensity and human tension, as well as looking at the same incidents from different perspectives to deepen meanings.

CONCLUSION

No two lessons are alike, and in teaching classroom drama this is more marked because of the improvisational nature of the medium. Added to this are the different personalities in your class (and you), and everyone's changing moods and outlook. This complexity is not negative however, it is a challenge for you to understand and use. You are already managing these differences minute by minute, day by day, but they do need to be reconsidered in managing your drama.

This resource book with its attendant structure and recommended plan in each chapter, may imply that there is one way to teach drama and that the lesson plans are to be implemented as written. However this is not our intention. The lessons are offered as suggestions, and constitute a framework within which you need to make your own selections and decisions as your drama unfolds. Like any well-prepared meal they ultimately rely upon the cook and the process of cooking! Your oven may be fiercely hot or easily controlled, only you know your class and you will need to adjust the 'cooking' times accordingly. Managing classroom drama relies upon knowledge and experience of the medium, as well as flexibility and a sensitive eye for observing the detail of what is going on amongst the children. It is a demanding, but energising medium of learning, which with careful planning can be effectively handled and responsively managed.

Chapter 16

DRAMA AND ENGLISH TIME

INTRODUCTION

Drama can make a significant contribution to the development of speaking and listening, reading and writing. Various drama conventions can be employed in English sessions to feed into shared reading and writing, and teaching objectives can be brought to life through dramatic exploration and increased interaction. Improvisation demands children's full involvement and this can energise the study of a text, and help the learners engage with the theme, the issue or the characters, enriching their understanding of the text in the process. The experience of drama can provide purpose and audience for writing, and create access to writing in a wide range of genres, including letters and reports, diaries and argument, leaflets and play scripts.

Teachers in KS2 can integrate drama conventions into the literacy hour and can also include classroom drama within their timetables. Such provision can, (alongside other planned speaking and listening opportunities), encompass NC statutory orders for ATI and develop children's imagination in action, as well as enrich their creative writing. In KS3, a planned drama curriculum may be timetabled separately from English, although in many schools it will be taught under the umbrella of English, by teachers whose first specialism is English. This does not prevent its inclusion in literacy lessons however.

Texts being studied in English represent useful resource material for full classroom drama. For example, whilst studying Nina Bawden's novel *Carrie's War* or Jaqueline Wilson's book *Cliffhanger*, the class can create elements of these in classroom drama, inventing the next chapter or a later scenario in the text, before they hear the author's version. Long novels can come to life through drama and other tales in the same genre, or with the same theme, can be created to widen the children's repertoire and build upon their textual knowledge. Alternatively, whilst focusing on the non-fiction writing of discussions for example, a class could explore in drama the implications of an out of town shopping scheme and produce newspaper articles debating and discussing the issue. In this way, classroom drama outside dedicated literacy time can be connected to it and can provide quality material for writing fiction and non fiction.

In addition, single drama conventions employed in English time can draw the learner into the text, extend their involvement and understanding and provide rich material for writing. In effect conventions are used for pre-writing, as an oral rehearsal for later written composition. To capitalise on such short-lived drama activities, undertaken for the purpose of text deconstruction or reconstruction, teachers need to help the children connect back to the text. Articulating what they've learnt about the characters, theme, plot or situation is important. For example, after the children have role played Rapunzel and the sorceress arguing about her imprisonment in the tower, the teacher needs to provide time for the class to discuss what they've learnt about the characters. A summary of their character traits could be listed and used in writing. Bridging discussions like these, between the drama convention and the text, give weight to and profile reflection of both the medium of drama and the form and content of the communication.

For less confident drama teachers and children inexperienced in drama, employing individual drama conventions in English can be a worthwhile introduction to their potential and help develop knowledge about dramatic forms, as well a richer understanding of the text. On returning to the text, new insights gained in drama can be tested out. Closer attention to the text and increased interest in it, is often fostered through dramatic engagement, which can also enhance children's voice and stance in their writing. A range of conventions can be used for text level work on comprehension and composition, many of which are noted in this chapter with examples to demonstrate this approach. Drama based activities suitable for independent work in English time are also briefly noted. It must be re-emphasised however, that on its own such work is not doing full justice to classroom drama, which needs time to unfold and should be given its own curriculum time. In addition, teachers must be wary of using drama as an inevitable precursor to writing.

Using Drama Conventions for Comprehension and Composition

INVESTIGATING STORY STRUCTURE

Predicting narrative action within a text, or examining previous scenarios is possible through the use of drama conventions in English, since in drama, time can be controlled. A number of conventions can aid the investigation of narrative structure.

1. *Improvisations or freeze frames* can be made to show predicted narrative events, either those expected immediately or later in the text. For example, the class can be given the remaining chapter titles in a novel and asked to create one significant event in a later chapter. This will involve small groups actively predicting and hypothesising possibilities, and portraying these. Their ideas could be recounted in shared writing as a paragraph, mapped out as a chapter plan or written as a play script of the scene. A single freeze frame could also be made by groups to show a highly significant moment in a text, which may in a short story, be the climax. For example, the climax of Alun Durant's *Angus Rides the Goods Train* could be shown and an additional paragraph written to flesh out this moment of climax and tension.

2. *Sequential freeze frames* can be created to show the beginning, the series of events in the middle of the narrative and the final scenario at the end. For example, simple sequential freeze frames could be made to summarise the story *Mufaro's Beautiful Daughters* by John Steptoe. In effect, the children physically make a corporate storyboard of the text, and a summary of the story is created. Titles can be given to the significant events shown in these freeze frames and each child could then select one event to record in written form as a paragraph in the text.

3.   *Flashbacks or flash-forwards* of scenes can be made to examine the relationship between the present, the past and the future. For example, during an early part of Leon Garfield's *Fair's Fair*, a flashback depicting Jackson and Lillipolly ten years earlier, could highlight their plight and the limited likelihood of change in their social and financial situation. This could be written up as a remembered episode or as a literary flashback, and integrated into the text in an appropriate place.

4.   *Retelling* in role one event in a text or the whole text, is another option for revisiting the story structure. For example, a park keeper, who is explaining his day to his wife, could retell the text of *Voices in the Park* by Anthony Browne. This will contrast with the four voices that tell their own tales and will undoubtedly highlight the issues examined in the text. The park keeper could also record his day in a diary entry that night.

INVESTIGATING CHARACTERS

Drama conventions can increase children's awareness of a character's behaviour, their motives, speech and emotions as well as establish their point of view in a text. Such imaginative work is more than valid in shared reading, as classes corporately develop their shared understanding of the character concerned. Through hot seating for example, the class will pose questions to a character and then share the insights gained. Shared and independent writing about characters can also be prompted through interactive drama activities in literacy time, in writing in role for example, as a particular character, a stance is adopted which can be pursued and developed through the writing.

1.   *Role play* in pairs or with the whole class and the teacher, can provide the chance to expand the text and build a sense of the characters through improvising conversations, which are non-existent or not fully developed in the story. In expanding the language of the unsaid, the children inhabit the character's perspective and voice their views. If this is recorded in writing, the piece may be charged with the emotions and experience of the drama. For example, in *Rats* by Pat Hutchins, the conversation between Sam, who desperately wants a rat for a pet, and his Mum, who cannot bear rats, can be improvised. In attempting to capture this in shared writing as dialogue in the text, discussion can focus initially upon the different character's views and attitudes, as well as the language of persuasion and later, the style of writing and elements of punctuation can be considered. When the class take up their roles again to read their shared writing together, they will bring it to life and as a result become more able to evaluate the quality of their writing.

2.   *Hot seating* a character provides an opportunity for the class to ask questions of them in role and find out more about a particular individual. For example in *The Lady of Shallot* by Alfred Lord Tennyson, the Lady herself, trapped in the Tower, could be hot seated (either with the teacher in role or with a small number of the class taking her role corporately). The rest of the class might take up the role of a visitor, her nurse or a maid. Even if little is revealed, questions about the text will be unravelled. Dialogue emerging from this convention might be captured in speech bubbles or as prose.

3.   *Decision alley* can be used to examine the advantages and disadvantages of situations from a particular character's point of view and highlight the complex nature of the decision to be made. For example in *Children of Winter* by Berlie Doherty, which is about the plague, Catherine, the eldest child is responsible for her siblings since they are separated from their parents. The children are starving, and seeing hens across the river in Eyam, Catherine has to decide whether to steal one or not. The class could make a decision alley for her to walk down and voice her thoughts, worries and conscience pricking concerns at this moment in the drama. Afterwards, the child who took up the role of Catherine, could be questioned about her decision, what views tipped the balance? Her thoughts could be recorded in two lists to support the reflective diary or letter writing which might emerge from this.

4. *Thought tracking* is considerably more demanding than responding to a teacher's questions about how a character feels, but it enables all the children to engage more fully with the character's perspectives. For example, in Laurence Anholt's *Cinderboy*, the class, on hearing how the hero is left at home for the Cup Final (in which his team, Royal Palace are playing), could simultaneously speak out loud the thoughts and feelings of the young footballer. In listening to their own words and voicing Cinderboy's views, the children will all be involved in being the character, albeit very briefly. The eventual list of words and phrases to describe his state of mind will be much more varied as a consequence of this engagement and are likely to be offered by a wider number of children. It may be helpful to group these words under particular emotions, as synonyms that the children might use in their own writing. Thought bubbles could capture the character's inner feelings generated through this convention, or a paragraph of prose could be constructed as an interior monologue to reflect their state of mind.

5. *Small group improvisation* can also help to develop a sense of various characters' perspectives in particular situations. For example in *The Wreck of the Zanzibar* by Michael Morpurgo, when Laura's brother goes missing, groups of children, as the family, could discuss the possible reasons for his disappearance. Following a reading of Morpurgo's passage dealing with this issue, the class could write in role as one of the family to explore the thoughts, feeling and views of their chosen character.

6. *Role play with thought tracking* is a challenging convention to develop in English time, but does highlight contradictions in what is said and what is thought in certain situations, so it reveals a lot about a character's inner emotions. Two children voice the inner thoughts of two characters aloud, during a role play which is being undertaken by two other children. Initially, it is helpful for a small group to model this. It is useful to explore the linguistic conventions of narrative asides, interior monologues and the use of irony in writing and helps to make explicit a character's inner tensions.

7. *Role on the wall* can be built up over time as a novel is read, and perspectives on one character can be recorded at different points in the text. It can also provide insight into a character's thinking, their values, feelings and attitudes. After a shared reading of the text, the class can write in the role on the wall, key lines, phrases, ideas or feelings about the character from the perspective of others. For example, in reading any of the *Harry Potter* books by J. K. Rowling, a role in the wall could be made of Harry, and information about him added over time. His uncle and aunt's views could also be noted as well as Harry's own self perception. This convention can be enriched through hot seating the character and summarising the knowledge or perceptions gained. The role on the wall can be used as a resource for writing about the character.

8. *Telephone conversations* can be improvised, either building upon a phone call in the text or as an entirely invented conversation. For example in *Bad Girls* by Jacqueline Wilson, the phone conversation between Mandy and Arthur King could be extended in action and then captured in collaborative writing, highlighting the relationship between them.

INVESTIGATING THEMES

The underlying theme of a text is a valuable area to examine through small group drama work. In using drama conventions to portray their understanding of the theme, the children can more easily develop their views and through observing other groups' interpretations, alternatives are more fully considered.

1. *Group sculptures* are useful conventions to convey themes. For example, in *Flour Babies* by Anne Fine, the class, having heard the book can be asked to make small group sculptures to signify a key issue in the tale. The collective construction of this sculpture will prompt the children to share their own understandings of the theme and evidence in the text can be quoted to support this view in writing. Such sculptures can also be titled, or summarised as proverbs to pinpoint the issue.

2. *Moment of truth* is a convention appropriately employed when a text is not quite complete, since each group devises a final scene for the story. For example, in Joyce Dunbar's *The Glass Garden* the children can show whether Lorenzo's precious daughter will remain imprisoned in glass forever. Their ideas for this final scene will take into account their understanding of earlier inference, and their improvisation can easily be written as an alternative ending in the style of the text.

3. *Interviews* between characters in the text can also be valuable to explore the relationship between characters and how they reflect the theme in words and actions. *In The Rascally Cake* by Jeanne Willis, Mr Rufus Skumskins O'Parsley is interviewed by a television journalist about the whereabouts of his rascally cake and its ingredients. After the interviews this could be turned into a news item about personal health, hygiene and morality, so the theme of the text is further examined in another genre.

4. *Forum theatre* is an improvisation performed by a few in the forum of the classroom. In interrupting and refining this, the rest of the class contribute. This is useful to explore issues in particular contexts. Playscripts can be built on the scene created, or if the observers are in role as trainee professionals, their reports and recommendations can be written.

5. *A whole class meeting* can be held to investigate an issue in a text and in effect the class improvise a response to a situation in the text, which can be drawn upon in writing. The *teacher in role*. The meeting may be a tribal council, a courtroom, a staff meeting at the factory, a family forum or whatever. For example, in Raymond Wilson's poem *This Letter's to Say*, the local council inform a family their house is to be knocked down, 'But your house will - we are pleased to say - be the fastest lane of the motorway'. A local council meeting can be set up, formal letters of complaint composed, and later the poem read again with increasing insight. For further details and a copy of the poem see Chapter 2.

Many of these conventions can also be used to explore non-literary texts. For example, improvisations of family discussions about television viewing could feed into discursive writing, or brief television adverts could be created to explore the subtle language of persuasion and influence. Magazine and newspaper reports can also be enriched by active dramatic engagement in the issue under consideration, and the seeds for play scripts are obviously best sown through interaction and improvisation.

Using Drama in Independent Work

Collaborative and imaginative drama activities represent valid independent work which can be related to teaching objectives and the children's own learning targets. Again, these will help children use a wider than usual range of spoken and written language and can focus closely on characters' words, their intonation, meaning and effect in particular contexts. A range of activities can be undertaken in pairs and groups, many of which will mirror the use of conventions in whole class shared reading and writing time and may follow up work begun in this context. These activities may need to be sustained over a couple of days in order to achieve the set objectives. The use of a tape recorder may help to focus small group oral work in independent work time, and ensuring that drama groups regularly feedback to the class in the plenary is also important. Activities could include the following.

- *Paired work in role*, emerging from fiction or non -fiction content, this can lead comfortably into collaborative writing of a scene in a book, an extract of a play script or a newspaper report.

- *Oral retelling in small groups* of a significant part of a tale can prompt taped retellings with a narrator and a full range of characters and sound effects.

- *Oral retelling in pairs* from one character's viewpoint can be prompted by an emotions graph, or whole class role on the wall work. This may lead into writing diary entries, letters or writing about the characters as the narrator of the text.

- *Small group improvisations* can be prepared to illuminate the relationship between particular characters or to examine more closely an important scene or issue. In the plenary, this improvisation could be used for presentation, reflection and debate, or as a piece of forum theatre, to which the class contribute through review, response and reconstruction.

CONCLUSION

Drama offers English teachers the chance to increase interaction and involvement in whole class contexts and develop children's affective engagement, as well as their personal response to the text. Expanding the repertoire of drama conventions used in English time can enrich practice, actively involve all the class and encourage the generation of ideas based on inferential evidence. Drama conventions can operate as effective precursors to shared writing since they generate ideas in action that can be reflected upon and captured in writing. In shared reading, this interactive approach allows more to be uncovered about the character, theme or plot and engages the children's imaginations in pursuit of further insights. In this way using drama conventions, however briefly, in working in English can encourage a closer examination of the text, bring fresh energy to the children's later encounters with it and reveal subtexts through the process of creating inference in action.

However, classroom drama still needs to be given its own curriculum time in order to more fully develop the emotional, imaginative, artistic, cognitive and linguistic competence of the children. Drama is much more than a tool to enhance language development and does not deserve to be trapped in English time and used merely as a prompt for speaking and listening, reading and writing.

Chapter 17
Drama Conventions

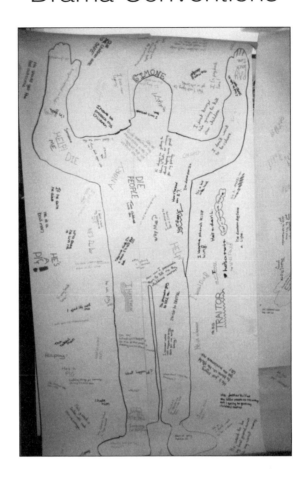

INTRODUCTION

A range of drama conventions exist, which can be utilised in classroom drama. Individually, each creates different demands and prompts particular kinds of thinking and interaction appropriate at certain moments in the drama. To use them effectively, you will need to become well acquainted with these conventions, so this chapter explores the nature and purpose of the major conventions, and provides examples to bring them to life. They are not, however, rigid structures and can be adapted to suit the dramatic exploration and used flexibly during the session. For convenience they are examined in alphabetical order.

Decision Alley

This convention refers to any situation in which there are different choices of action, conflicting interests or dilemmas. It is useful to examine the pros and cons of a decision. Two lines of children face each other, approximately two paces apart and reasonably spaced out. One child in role walks slowly down the alley between them. As this character progresses down the alley, their thoughts or the sets of views for and against a course of action, which the role faces, are voiced out loud by the rest of the class. The character can then be hot seated at the end of the alley, to establish their final decision and to understand why they have made this choice. For example, in a World War Two drama, a mother may have to decide whether her sick child should be evacuated, her thoughts and views can be voiced so that the complexity of her decision is revealed.

Drawing in Role

This involves the children individually or in small groups drawing a significant object in the drama. For example, a detailed drawing of some particular flora and fauna found during the migration west of the American pioneers can help children invent possibilities and ideas for future action. In this way the drawing enhances the drama and creates new meanings.

Flashback / Flashforward

This involves the class in exploring some event in a character's past or future, or conjecturing what might be happening simultaneously elsewhere. This device can be equated with the fast forward / rewind on the video player, although the portrayal might be undertaken as a freeze frame or as an improvisation. Flashbacks seek to explain a character's current behaviour, whilst flash forwards seek to examine the consequences of recent events. For example, a flash forward might show the situation in the village, ten years after the events, which the drama examined.

Forum Theatre

This is an improvisation performed by a few members of the class in the forum of the classroom, which is then discussed, revisited and developed. In its simplest form, an important situation is improvised and watched by the class, and the words and actions of those involved are commented upon, (with the helpful mediation of the teacher) and then the same situation is reworked taking into account what has been said. A development of this technique is to offer the children, actors or observers, the chance to stop the action, suggest changes and justify their alternative ideas. This convention allows the drama to be revisited, making use of many of their ideas. It is valuable for examining difficult situations more closely and working out how they might best be tackled. For example, in a drama based upon *The Iron Man* by Ted Hughes, the children may have to deal with the scientist who made him, and this interaction could well be tricky for them to negotiate successfully. Using this convention would give them a chance of coaching each other during interchanges, in a way which makes their negotiation with the scientist more successful.

Freeze Frame

This convention is also known as creating tableaux, still images or statue making. Individually, in small groups or as a whole class, the children use their bodies to create an image of an event, an idea, a theme or a moment in time. This still, silent picture freezes the action, as do newspaper photographs, but it can also portray a visual memory, or a wish, or show an image from a dream, as well as represent more abstract themes such as anger, jealousy or truth. For example, in a drama about the Mayflower, the children can make freeze frames showing the Pilgrim Fathers departing from England. Freeze frames can also be brought to life, and can be subtitled with an appropriate caption, written or spoken, or have noises and sound effects added to them. In addition, the words or inner thoughts of members of the tableau can be voiced when the teacher touches children on the shoulder. Freeze frames offer a useful way of capturing and conveying meaning, since groups can convey much more than they would be able to through words alone.

Group Sculpture

This is closely allied to freeze-frame, since the group make a sculpture to express a particular aspect of a theme or the issue being examined. These tend to be abstract and non-representational in nature and prompt the children to share their own perceptions of underlying themes. For example, at the close of a drama about the Kosovan crisis, group sculptures can seek to convey the themes examined in the drama, e.g. fear, oppression, human vunerability.

Hot Seating

In this convention, the teacher and/or the children assume the role of one or more individuals from the drama and are questioned by the remainder of the class. The class need to be forewarned and primed to think of questions. They can ask the questions either as themselves, so their point of view is outside the drama, or they can adopt a role within the drama and ask questions from this perspective. If the class is in role, this helps to focus the kind of questions asked and may prompt the need for notes to be taken. For example, in a drama about *Harry Potter and the Philosopher's Stone* by J. K. Rowling, neighbours of the Dursleys might put Uncle Vernon and Aunt Petunia on the hot-seat and question them about their treatment of young Harry. Several characters from the drama can be placed on the hot seat at once, or alternatively a single character on the hot seat can be represented by two or more children, this provides security for whoever is on the hot seat. This is a useful probing technique which seeks to develop knowledge of the character's motives, attitudes and behaviour. It encourages increased reflective awareness of the complex nature of human behaviour.

Improvisation: small group

Improvisation can be prepared beforehand or spontaneously developed. In the former small groups of children, discuss, plan and then create a piece of prepared improvisation. This kind of improvisation is relatively secure, because through their discussion they create a kind of script or structure to follow. For example, in a drama about Guy Fawkes small groups can improvise the plotting, or his eventual arrest and interrogation. Alternatively, the dramatic scene can be spontaneously improvised by the group, who make it up as they speak and respond to one another in role. This requires more confidence, but is more rewarding because it reflects actual living and the communicative demands which are faced second by second. It also provides access to children's unconscious pre-occupations, which are invaluable to the teacher. Some groups of learners hold back from spontaneous improvisation whilst others pitch straight into role, all children need the opportunity to experience both kinds of improvisation.

Improvisation: whole class

The whole class, including the teacher, engage in improvisation together. Again such improvisation can be planned or spontaneous. It can be 'formal' as in a whole class meeting, for example, a court scene, or more informal, an improvisation of a market scene, shortly before a major incident occurs. Whole class role play reduces the pressure of being watched since everyone is corporately engaged and lives in the moment, responding to each other naturally in the imaginary context. The teacher in role frequently takes a critical role in whole class improvisation.

Maps / Diagrams

Together the class make a large collective map or diagram of an area or the scene of a crime. This can help establish a corporate sense of place, and provides a concrete reference for the events which take place there. Alternatively, groups can produce small maps or diagrams to show more detail about the context. Such visuals often move the drama on, as possible elements are identified through the drawing and their place in the unfolding events are examined or retained for later use. For example, drawing a diagram of the new indoor leisure centre allows many future possibilities related to place, character and incident to be imagined.

Mantle of the Expert

This convention involves children being given, or adopting roles, which necessarily include the expertise, authority, knowledge and skills of specialists. Their expertise is explicitly used in the drama. This knowledge may be recently acquired from classroom research, or it might be their own personal expertise, but the status it gives the children, allows them to significantly influence the drama. The teacher must honour their expertise and may therefore take on a role of relative ignorance in the drama, or assume a more equal role alongside them. This general technique, developed by Dorothy Heathcote, is very empowering for learners since considerable responsibility is given to the class and insight can be gained into different occupations. For example, children can take up roles as historians and archaeologists researching a site and using their knowledge to promote and publicise the site, handling challenges along the way.

Mime

This convention ranges from simple whole class mime, in which each child mimes the relevant actions supported by their teacher/narrator, to more refined small group mime and the crafted use of gesture, facial expression and body movement. It is useful to establish an imaginary context and does remove the pressure of dialogue, although in a moment of stillness the teacher can prompt the sharing of the mimed character's inner thoughts by asking them to speak their thoughts out loud. It is also valuable for allowing violence to be represented in a controlled fashion, for example, in miming the knights stealthily creeping up on Thomas à Beckett, in Canterbury Cathedral.

Moment of Truth

This convention is useful for resolving a drama and prompts discussion of the suggested events in the final scene. Usually a small group will create this scene for the rest of the class, not in order to entertain but in order to draw together their understanding of the drama and create a truthful representation of the likely reality. This is discussed by the whole class and the scene may be replayed to try out alternative versions until the class are satisfied that the moment is truthful. For example, in a drama which explores the consequences of parental pressure and high expectations, the group might finally try out different ways of portraying the teenager's attempt to raise the issue with his/her parents.

Narration

This convention relates to the teacher, or children as storytellers. In the former, the teacher can offer narrative links or a running commentary alongside the drama which can give coherence and widen perspectives. For instance, while a group enact a school scene, the teacher might offer alternative narrations highlighting the child's story, the teacher's story and the friend's story. In the latter, child narrators can describe their group's mime, giving atmosphere and adding tension and shape to the drama.

Objects

Objects can be useful in drama as they imply actions, events and people, as well as extend meanings which are being built up by the teacher. Through symbolising attitudes, values and relationships they can help establish a character's role and subtly state information about them, which is not easily said in words. For example, using a key as a symbol of a guarded possession, or an axe as a potential weapon in the hands of an apparently friendly visitor. Such objects operate as wordless metaphors.

Overheard Conversations

In small groups, conversations between characters are improvised, and then a few are 'overheard' by the class to add tension and information, and to enable a range of viewpoints to be established. The group can also recreate key conversations from the past that shed light upon the present situation. The teacher as storyteller may later integrate these perspectives into the drama. For example, in *Ladder to the Sky* by Barbara Esbensen, a member of a tribe seems particularly blessed by the gods, causing others to become jealous and begin to spread gossip and rumours about him. These might be overheard by his grandmother or a friend.

Play Making

Using this convention, small groups plan, practice and present extremely short improvisations, which might be flashbacks or flashforwards in the life of a character in the community or might express alternative courses of action in the present. These are useful for sequencing ideas and developing confidence in performance. For example, making a brief play-let based upon the expectations of the next chapter in *The Wreck of the Zanzibar* by Michael Morpurgo.

Ritual or Ceremony

In ritual, the teacher and the class together work out ways of marking significant events in the narrative and create some form of ceremony which is part of the drama. Such rituals often slow the drama down and provoke a deepening sense of significance, as well as reflection. For example, the children as villagers might create a chant or simple dance to thank their gods for their beneficence, or in another drama, different villagers might write prayers and make artefacts to leave at the burial site of their shaman. Ritual is often used to conclude work or to intensify the tenor of a drama.

Role on the Wall

In this convention, an outline is drawn around an important character as they lie upon a large piece of paper, and then information and feelings about the character are written into the shape by each child. This can be added to throughout the drama. It can also be enriched by being written from different perspectives, for example, the space outside the outline can contain comments about the character as they are seen from an observer's viewpoint and the interior space can contain the character's own thoughts and point of view. For example, in exploring the life of a missing child, the group can, as the drama progresses, add a series of statements made about her, by her parents, teacher, friends, and her own point of view can be noted inside the role outline. This is a valuable convention for building a deeper understanding of a chosen role.

Sound Tracking/Collage

This convention involves sounds being made, via the voice, body or through other percussion instruments to evoke atmosphere and express meaning in a musical collage. The sounds can be made to accompany action or a freeze frame, or to create an environment in sound, either way they encourage children to experiment and convey mood expressively. For example, the sound effects of a rising storm or the noise made in a factory working flat out for a deadline, can be composed and 'played', either in small groups or by the whole class.

Teacher in Role

This is the most powerful convention the teacher has at their disposal. It involves the teacher engaging fully in the drama by taking various roles. This technique is a tool through which the teacher can support, extend and challenge the children's thinking from inside the drama. The teacher in role can influence events from within the developing situation. Every role has its own social status which gives access to an influence commensurate with its position. High status roles have a controlling and deciding nature, whilst lower status roles are not so openly powerful, but can still be influential. For example, a high status role would be a Pharoah or the Captain of a ship, whilst a lower status role would be a servant in the Pharoah's temple or a stowaway on board. For teachers beginning to use this technique, it is helpful to forewarn the class that you are going into role, and then pause a while before beginning. Whilst in role try not to lose your concentration or come out of role, if you do, they will also, children value their teacher's commitment and reciprocate in kind.

Teacher as Storyteller

This convention involves the teacher using narration to provide structure and coherence, to link action, mark the passage of time or reflect upon a character's perspective or deepen the significance and meaning of events. The teacher can, through careful narration build atmosphere, change the pace and give form and shape to the dramatic activity. If the tale is told and retold as a drama unfolds, then the teacher can include the children's ideas as part of the narrative. This is significant as it honours their ideas and ensures *their* story is told. This device can be used throughout the drama or just at a few significant moments to introduce, to link or to conclude the drama. It is a particularly useful tool in drama sessions with younger children.

Telephone Conversations

This can involve the children in pairs, improvising the conversation between two characters on the phone at a certain point in the drama. Alternatively, the teacher in role can hold a one way telephone conversation on an imaginary telephone and prompt the class to infer the other half of the conversation. This is a useful device for passing on important information, for letting time pass and recollecting the events of the period, and it can also add tension to situations. For example, in *Carrie's War* by Nina Bawden, Carrie could telephone her mother to tell her about her new 'home'.

Thought Tracking

In this convention, the private thoughts of individuals are shared publicly. This can be organised in different ways; the teacher can touch individuals on the shoulder during a freeze-frame, or halt an improvisation and ask them to voice their thoughts. Or the whole class can take on the persona of one individual and simultaneously speak out loud their thoughts and fears in a particular situation. Alternatively the teacher, or a child in role, can give witness to the class and speak personally about recent events from a 'special' chair, or members of the class can take turns in moving forward to stand behind an empty chair and express their thoughts about a character which the chair represents. For example, in a drama in which a character has been turned to ice, as in *The Ice Palace* by Robert Swindells, the class could make a circle around an empty chair, or a motionless child, and take it in turns to come forward to touch the stone child and express their inner thoughts and fears. This convention is useful to slow down the action and can prompt both a deeper understanding of individual characters and sensitive responses to what has happened.

Word Play/ Choral Chanting

This is useful to add mood and evoke atmosphere, it involves the children in creating word patterns, phrases or chants which can be repeated or intoned within the drama. For example in a drama, which potentially has marching feet, such as a drama about the Luddites going to a factory, some words or phrases could be composed to be chanted in time with the feet on the move. Such work has a poetic nature and evokes different perspectives and moods. Alternatively, the teacher could offer a few lines or verses from a poem, which can be repeated or experimented with in order to intensify a theme in the drama, for example the title. *This is the House that Crack Built* by Clark Taylor, could be repeated alongside freeze frames of a character in a drug rehabilitation centre.

Writing in Role

A variety of kinds of writing can emerge from the lived experience of the drama and can be written in role, eg, letters, diaries, messages, pamphlets, notes, even graffiti. For example, in a drama about opening a local tourist shop, a multitude of forms of writing may be involved, including adverts for jobs, fliers about the shop, interior designs, letters of information to the press, display resumés, as well as the diaries of the workers, newspaper reports, scripts for a radio item on the shop, and so on. Children often write with considerable urgency in drama since they are emotionally engaged they have a purpose and a clearly imagined audience for their writing. For example, in a drama about a trip to an adventure centre, one child challenged in various ways on the first day, may begin a letter home written in the secrecy of their bed, such *writing in role* occurs during the drama. After the close of the drama, *writing related to role* may also take place when, from a distance just outside the drama, newspaper accounts, letters, arguments, discussions and debates in magazines, and thank you notes for example may be written.

CONCLUSION

None of these conventions are fixed and unchangeable, you'll find you can change them to suit your purposes, adapting them to the needs of the drama, and if you create new ones for yourself so much the better. They are not rules. Some conventions have in-built opportunities for performance, which need to be used cautiously, particularly small group improvisation. If you are not careful a great deal of valuable time can be taken up with groups preparing play-lets, and then sitting and watching one another. A small amount of this is justified, but the watching becomes far more valuable if it is purposefully used in the context of a wider drama and a variety of conventions are used to construct meaning. Drama conventions help shape the meaning of the text under construction. They need to be employed appropriately to open up the imaginary world, create the characters and situations and investigate the issues lying beneath the text.

FURTHER READING

If you would like to read more about teaching drama we recommend the following books which discuss both theory and practice in the context of the classroom.

Booth, D. (1994) *Story Drama: Reading, Writing and Role Playing across the Curriculum*, Ontario, Pembroke.

Griffiths, J. (1991) *An Early Start to Drama*, Herts, Simon and Schuster.

Heathcote, D. and Bolton, G. (1995) *Drama for Learning*, Portsmouth, Heinemann.

Kitson, N. and Spiby, I. (1997) *Drama 7-11 : Developing Primary Teaching Skills*, London, Routledge.

Neelands, J. and Goode, T. (2000) *Structuring Drama Work - A Hand Book of Available Forms in Theatre and Drama* (New Edition), Cambridge. Cambridge University Press.

Neelands, J. (1998) *Beginning Drama 11-14*, London, David Fulton.

O'Neill, C. (1995) *Drama Worlds: A Framework for Process Drama*, Portsmouth, NH, Heinemann.

Readman, G. and Lamont, G. (1994) *Drama: A Handbook for Primary Teachers*, London, BBC.

Taylor, K. (ed) (1991) *Drama Strategies: New Ideas from Drama*, Oxford, Heinemann.

Winston, J. (1998) *Drama, Narrative and Moral Education*, London, Falmer Press.

Winston, J. and Tandy, M. (1998) *Beginning Drama 4-11*, London, David Fulton.

Nate Drama Committee (2000) *Cracking Drama, Progression in Drama within English 5-16*, Sheffield, NATE.